What Saves Us

WHAT SAVES US

Poems of Empathy and Outrage in the Age of Trump

Edited by
MARTÍN ESPADA

CURBSTONE BOOKS / NORTHWESTERN UNIVERSITY PRESS
EVANSTON, ILLINOIS

Curbstone Books
Northwestern University Press
www.nupress.northwestern.edu

The editor and the publisher have made every reasonable effort to contact copyright holders to obtain permission to use the material reprinted in this book. Acknowledgments are printed starting on page 247, which should be considered an extension of this copyright page.

10 9 8 7 6 5 4 3 2 1

Library of Congress Cataloging-in-Publication Data

Names: Espada, Martín, 1957– editor.
Title: What saves us : poems of empathy and outrage in the age of Trump / edited by Martín Espada.
Description: Evanston, Illinois : Curbstone Books / Northwestern University Press, 2019.
Identifiers: LCCN 2019018546 | ISBN 9780810140776 (trade paper : alk. paper) | ISBN 9780810140837 (e-book)
Subjects: LCSH: Political poetry, American—21st century. | United States—Politics and government—2017—Poetry. | American poetry—21st century. | LCGFT: Political poetry.
Classification: LCC PS595.P634 W48 2019 | DDC 811.608035873933—dc23
LC record available at https://lccn.loc.gov/2019018546

Contents

Preface: The Filthy Presidentiad
Martín Espada

November 2018: There is a caravan of Central American migrants straggling through México on a pilgrimage to a place they pray will save them. The president of the United States promises to send thousands of federal troops to the border to halt what he calls an "invasion," claiming, without evidence, that terrorists and criminals march with the families hauling infants. He authorizes these troops to fire on anyone who throws rocks, equating pebbles with bullets. The first troops have arrived at the border, rifles bristling, despite the fact that the caravan is hundreds of miles away. Meanwhile, migrant children taken from their parents at the border languish in makeshift prison camps.

This is not a novel. This is not a dystopian fantasy. This is our country under the regime of Donald J. Trump.

Trump announced his candidacy in June 2015, with the pronouncement that Mexicans crossing the border brought with them, like the plague, a range of criminal tendencies, from drug smuggling to rape. In August 2015, two brothers, Scott and Steve Leader, took him at his word, attacking a homeless Mexican immigrant sleeping outside a subway stop in Boston, urinating in his face to wake him up, then breaking his nose. Scott told police, "Donald Trump was right. All these illegals need to be deported." More than three years later, millions of people believe that Donald Trump is right about everything.

This is an anthology of poems in the Age of Trump—and much more than Trump. To be sure, there are poems about Trump and his pathological demagoguery, or that rose in the throat of the poet the day after his election, some in mourning, some organizing the next protest.

More broadly, however, these are poems that either *embody* or *express* a sense of empathy or outrage in the Age of Trump, both prior to and following his election, since it is empathy the president lacks and outrage he provokes as a result. These are poems that confront the culture and values of Trump, even if they predate his regime. (Poets have been writing about, and against, the culture of Trump for years, long before his name became a symbol for the destructive forces with which he is now synonymous.) These are poems that speak from the heart of the communities most gravely endangered in our times, or on behalf of these communities, poems that reflect the unstoppable diversification of this society, poems that assert our common humanity in the face of dehumanization.

The title of this anthology, *What Saves Us*, comes from a poem by Vietnam veteran Bruce Weigl. Fittingly, the poem turns on an act of empathy for a boy going to war. Here is one of Trump's beloved veterans, who bears witness to his reality, contradicting the cynical political fantasy. Here, too, in this anthology is Trump's beloved working class—even a former coal miner—speaking in voices that bear no resemblance to the voices we hear at Trump rallies and in the media.

There is an extraordinary multiplicity of voices. These voices speak of immigrants, persecuted and scapegoated. Immigrants themselves speak. (A Haitian poet, for example, rebuts the "shithole country" theory.) Even the Río Grande speaks of immigration. Other voices bear witness to police brutality against African Americans, to the innocent neighborhood eccentric shot down or strategies to stay alive. More voices speak of violence in all its manifestations, from gun violence at a primary school to violence against women and trans people everywhere, or of the indoctrination of violence that must be uprooted within us. Still more voices speak of poverty, the waitress surviving on leftovers at the restaurant, the battles of a teacher in a shelter for homeless mothers, the emergency room doctor, in broken sonnets, returning the narrative to the suffering human being. There are voices of labor, in the factory or the fields. There are voices from the epidemic of incarceration, unfolding in the letter a father sends a son. There are prophetic voices, imploring us to see ourselves reflected in the mirror of history, to grasp the gravity of the situation, to imagine the world we will leave behind in ruins lest we speak and act.

However, this is not simply a collection of grievances or denunciations. The poets build bridges. One poet walks the streets of the city and sees her immigrant past in the immigrant present. Another poet steps up to translate in Arabic at the airport for a lost stranger, Muslim travel ban be damned. Yet another declaims a musical manifesto after the hurricane that devastated his island. Yet another evokes a demonstration in the street, shouting in an ecstasy of defiance, embodying the joy of resistance.

In the Age of Trump, the hyper-euphemism "alternative facts" justifies official lies and "alt-right" refers to what everyone, even its apologists, once called "white supremacy." The poets in this collection have the compulsion and the capacity to take back the language, resisting the corruption of words themselves, repudiating deliberate obfuscation in the service of power. These poets take on the task of documenting the historical moment—and the more astonishing the moment, the more surreal or ominous, the more we need the poets to capture that moment in brushstrokes of language, to ground us in the present or to leave behind a record for future generations, who will ask: *What happened? What did you do?*

Three of the poets—Sam Hamill, Donald Hall, and Adrian Louis—have died since they contributed their poems to this anthology. All three knew that their lives might be nearing an end, yet they sent in work. Such was their urgency. This anthology owes a debt to Hamill's *Poets against the War*, an eloquent reply to the lethal madness in Iraq.

As we celebrate the bicentennial of Walt Whitman's birth in 2019, we should recall his fury in the poem "To the States": "What a filthy Presidentiad!" Whitman's jeremiad refers to President Franklin Pierce, but his words of outrage resonate as if he penned them today. So, too, do the words of hope and faith in that the same poem: "With gathering murk, with muttering thunder and lambent shoots we all duly awake."

What Saves Us

Elizabeth Alexander
Smile

When I see a black man smiling
like that, nodding and smiling
with both hands visible, mouthing

"Yes, Officer," across the street,
I think of my father, who taught us
the words "cooperate," "officer,"

to memorize badge numbers,
who has seen black men shot at
from behind in the warm months north.

And I think of the fine line—
hairline, eyelash, fingernail paring—
the whisper that separates

obsequious from *safe*. Armstrong,
Johnson, Robinson, Mays.
A woman with a yellow head

of cotton-candy hair stumbles out
of a bar at after-lunchtime
clutching a black man's arm as if

for her life. And the brother
smiles, and his eyes are flint
as he watches all sides of the street.

Julia Alvarez
Refugee Women

I

These women without countries,
these widows from Salvador,
these matchstick dreamers, these quick-bone
little sisters from Cambodia,
these somber Argentine matrons,
endless pampas on their faces—
where are we going to put them?
Isabel, Margarita,
Yoeum, Yat, Alicia,
and almond-pretty Sunhee?
The men are mostly dead,
Fernando and Francisco,
hurled in the holes they dug.
(They can hardly call it a burial.)
Now they're the crusted soil
these women scrape from their soles
on the welcome mats of our doorsteps.
Widowed, orphaned, exiled—
countless times they've been violated.
(What accounts are being kept?)
Their hands are fists in the pockets
of old housedresses we donated,
their smiles always the startle
of politeness on their faces.
Some are lucky with a child,
a snapshot distorted from folding;
some are unmarked; some are missing
only teeth and a few hours
when they blanked out in a cell
under penal interrogations
of a dozen guardias' hard-ons.
(We are glad their stories come
to us mostly in translation.)

II

Mothers, daughters, sisters
and girlfriends to the dead—
these women without countries
get through Customs with their ghosts
and haunt our United States.
We exorcise them with kindness.
Volunteers, we teach them how
to survive in their new country.
And they who have known the rod,
dry ice, gray rats, live wire,
grow humble before our stores,
our shopping malls, our outlets,
racks upon racks of clothes
in the sizes of their loved ones.
But however much we try
transforming them, they are never
quite saying what they mean,
never into the church picnics
the benefits and the rallies.
Each cart loaded with groceries,
each bundle of contributions
enough to feed & clothe a small village,
each thank you and goodbye
practiced before a mirror
so the face does not betray
the slightest hint of ingratitude—
is the surplus symptomatic
of the greed that makes a guardia.

III

Isabel, Yoeum, Yat,
Margarita, Amelia, Sunhee,
how will you survive
in this country club of a country,
remember but not recall
the dead you left behind you,
the silky limbs of a lover,
the small bundle of a child,
how the body empties of self

5

at the moment of violation?
You who have not yet arrived
to the warm brown of your bodies,
to the names we hope will recall you:
Alicia, Amelia, Yoeum,
Sunhee, Yat, Margarita.
Answer us, are you with us?
Did we rescue you in time?
Isabel and Alicia!
We have put you up in our houses,
taught you to use our language,
our money, our public transport,
where to sign, who to let in.
But by the blank in your eyes,
your smiles faint like old scars
on the emptiness of your faces,
we know you did not survive
the dead you carry inside you.

IV

They move inside our houses,
these dead with the dead inside them,
in our hand-me-downs, apologizing
in broken English, thanking us
for this sweater, this slice of ham,
this Barbie doll for a daughter.
On the news, they watch for faces
of a cousin or compadre.
But everyone looks familiar
on this telecast of the holocaust.
Our journalists bear witness
holding microphones to fresh corpses.
We try to keep count of death
with an abacus of conscience
repeating their names like prayers:
Yoeum, Yat, Amelia,
Margarita, Alicia, Sunhee . . .

Doug Anderson
Binge

War comes to visit me once a day.
I can't get rid of him.
He's grown old and hates himself.
I stopped a quarter-century ago,
but he still drinks—sits in airport bars
and watches the cocky uniforms
line up at the departure gates.
Desert camouflage this time, tan boots.
He orders another double and snickers,
little eyes set close together
in too large a head, like a grizzly's,
opaque and dead. Flies swarm
around his gore-smeared muzzle.
He stinks of corpse. I let him sleep in the garage.
You see, there's no way to make him leave.
Go to war just once, he's always with you.
At breakfast he feels like he's got
an ice pick in his head, swears off the stuff.
Never again, he says, I've found God.
By five he's back in the blood glow of the bar,
bumming drinks and telling lies.
He's got an eye for boys and girls
with wallets full of combat pay.
He'll Mickey Finn them,
roll them for their souls and go off giggling.
I see Senator Goldmouth weaving
down the bar to slap him on the back:
Let freedom ring! says he,
teeth twinkling from the neon at the bar.

Doug Anderson
How Nazis

The man in the driver's seat of the minivan is just short of backhanding his wife
but screams instead. The contractor towing a backhoe shouts at a man
who has crossed against the light. A man leans on his horn because the woman
in front of him is not turning fast enough. The weather is warm
and their windows are open and we can hear everything. Once again
the indifferent machine is closing on the soft human flesh it feeds on.
It is not 1930 and people are not yet cutting steaks from the draft horse
that has fallen in the streets, are not yet rolling a wheelbarrow
of deutschmarks to buy a loaf of bread. At the factory, a boss rides a machinist
until he quits, having no other job to go to. The machinist gets drunk
on the way home and his wife shouts at him and he hits his wife and the wife
hits the daughter and the daughter goes down the street where there is heroin.
A man sits in his room all day with his demons and talks to them.
They have been fouling their cages. They have been jeering at his dreams.
He goes to the basement and loads his assault rifle and then emerges
from his cave and you know the rest. The politicians scan
the surface for the bubbles of rage coming up from below, sing their
feral songs of blame and wrong and create phalanxes of hate.
They trot out the usual suspects: foreigners, people of color, homosexuals,
artists, and anyone who presents in this batholith of hate
a vision that is indigestible by the machine and whose songs
do not rhyme with the hard bells being rung to rally legions.
We are at the cusp of the eternal return one more time and the momentum
headed toward the cliff is terrifying. Those who do not join are dragged along.
Here is where God might step in but does not, once more,
stays in the shadows of the scaffolds being thrown up in every town square.

Doug Anderson
Subterranean Inner Redneck Blues

I got redneck in me goes way back, mixed with Swedes & Welsh
from up in Nebraska and if you believe my mad Irish grandmother,

some Indian. Everybody wants to have some Indian in them
and this must make Indians chuckle because even if I did

have some Indian in me I don't know shit about being Indian.
But that redneck is sure busy these days, trying to find

some kind of way to talk to people who are just this side
of a lynch-mob. I mean, I got brains and eggs and grits

but we learned most of that from black folks who had to do
the cooking so the pink-cheeked missus wouldn't soil her dress.

And I got some serious delta blues somewhere in me
and you know where maybe that comes from but nobody talks

about that, and when I was younger I thought maybe we had
some Jews in the family—my grandfather was named Wiseman—

but then I found out that could be English and besides
if you trace us back far enough you'll find he was

descended from *Wisermans*. But at that time they were
living on an Indian reservation in Mississippi, how about that?

Cree or Creek or Choctaw but nobody knows for sure.
I don't *know* any of this and now I find out

the blood tests don't tell you all that much. But I know
those rednecks rattling their chains back in some sharecropper

misery from when slavery was dismantled and they had to do
all the jobs the slaves had done   had to eat beans and lard, too.

My grandparents lived in a two-room shack
on the Mississippi bluffs in Hickman, Kentucky.

How you like that name—Hickman? But that old house is gone,
left a concrete foundation with the rust-stain of the old

woodstove my grandmother cooked three meals a day on.
Shared a garden with black folks down the hill,

man named Totten and his family—all equally miserable
during the Depression, grandfather working in the coal mines.

I don't know why they didn't get it then but by the time
they moved to Memphis it was back to N-word this,

N-word that, all the damn day long   but I think the hate
and hurt came from some deep booze-soaked place

and they just needed somebody to pin it on. Hate is like
stomping on a nest of fire ants, watch them

swarm up your leg. Anyhow, this is about how
my inner redneck has become troublesome these days

of out-of-the-closet racists strutting their stuff.
It's not good. I'd disown them if I could but I can't help

owning that DNA. What to do with it is the game:
I could say, I remember my grandmother's barbecue lamb

would bring folks from miles away, and that pile of cornbread,
bowl of collards, or how she'd go in the backyard

and snatch a chicken by the head, wring its neck, pluck it
and have it on the table with giblet gravy in a single afternoon.

I'm so old I remember when white people still won boxing matches.
I'd sit on the couch and watch with my grandfather, root for the black guy

just to piss him off. But then Floyd Patterson knocked out
Ingemar Johansson and that was it for white folks in the ring.

And then I went to that damn war that should have never happened.
And it was all, *I was so scared I didn't know whether to shit or go blind,*

and I put rednecks and black men equally in body bags
when I couldn't stop the bleeding. When a man's lips

are turning blue you know he may die, but listen,
you have to pull back a black man's lower lip to see

the cyanosis. They all died, were maimed, for a bunch
of fat liars in DC. We all rot in the earth the same way.

I wish to fuck I knew what to say to this redneck
who keeps popping up when I'm, you know, trying

to figure out why binaries are so often wrong, and
the mental constructions that we've made are pretty much

all bullshit. But here we are. There's that part Indian, maybe
part black trying to be all white getting up in my face

trying to get me to step across to the wrong side
with those Nazi mutherfuckers. Naw, I won't.

But I know how miserable all you sorry asses are.
How deep down you think not even that blue-eyed

velvet-painting Jesus will come through in the end.
I know your suffering, just wish to fuck

you knew what to do with it.
Grow a flower on a pile of shit. That may be it.

Naomi Ayala
Vending

Every night the patient gathering.
White compound bucket
full of black umbrellas
for 10 days of grey with no rain.
Caps, totes, sunglasses
the foldable, cherry red director's chair:
blue tarp bundles back of the minivan.
Day done at eight.
Duct-tape up the side-view mirror now
in K Street traffic singe.
The dank manifest, the night
holding tightly to its purse.

Naomi Ayala
They Roll the Tarp

Over the tool truck bed
unfurling the blue morning
move as if winter didn't weigh down on the body.
Markets could fall and do their dead cat dance
and they would be willing and able
to put in the decorative cabbage, the mums
clean up the sidewalk afterwards
return to dreams of *maybe tomorrow when* . . .
For now, they move near the front stoop trails
of rat excrement and pedestrian refuse
make way with shovels and pots
causing rats to take to tunnels, squirrels
to disperse among the coal-black bones
of trees on the block, till one of them lifts
his head from the hedgerow—daughter stopping by
in Sunday best, newborn at the shoulder
—to say how glad he is
his wife gave him the sight of her
black curls in the wild air
so he could be a grandfather today
among these men.

Benjamin Balthaser
Ghazal for Jim Foley #5: What Comes Home

Were you free then all along, Jim, free at last . . . ?
—ADRIENNE RICH, from *Ghazals: Homage to Ghalib* (1968)

The vanishing point where your bodies appear,
A desert horizon where nothing but light comes

Into being. I sit with two letters, one from a
Journalist and another from a soldier, overcome

With the heat and the violence. "*We killed 137 people
And a dog,*" B writes, "*all but the dog had it coming*

To them." From Jim: "*A picture is a way to structure suffering;
You cannot capture it but you can keep reality from coming*

Apart." Last night on the South Side I saw a body slumped
In the back seat of a police car as two cops waved the oncoming

Traffic to pass on by. I let the scene pass. The horizon
Where I see both your hands aiming a camera and a gun comes

To almost seem identical: bodies fall into line, seized
By acts of capture. I move on in ways so unencumbered

By the weights of your discoveries. Jim, I do not
Know where your body is buried. I cannot come

To terms with this. In the same way I cannot unsee B drive
The aimless hours into the dark: bodies that cannot come

Home. I hold your two letters the way I hold my two
Countries in my heart: what we must and will never overcome.

Sean Bates
The Face I Wore

I don't have all the letters
he wrote,
in a county jail, for me.
I have what I have
on yellow paper with attempts
at richer words. In the margin,
I see him try out *sesion, seshion,*
session, I love you, how's your mom? I know
his words written
in a caricature of the usual
scratches, he slows at a word, questions
the legibility. Do I see
a boy in this bed? Was it me
who bobbed and floundered, or him
who swam with what to say
and thrashed when I would
not write back.
Luxuriating evil in my stomach,
the power of silence.

Jan Beatty
Trumpcare

Hurt my leg in a fall,
think I need a wrap or X-ray,
but the white coat wants to prescribe Paxil.
He's writing a script, looking at his white pad,
I'm looking at his clean-cut dark hair, his
boxy glasses moving and changing,
blurring him into an animal head
or a politician.
I think this will help, he says.
What's my diagnosis? I say.
I didn't ask for medication, just told him about
my leg, my 57-cents-on-the-dollar body,
a woman-making-½-what-a-man-makes body—
he never looks up, says:
Take one of these at night.
Should I get an X-ray for my leg? I say,
his head now a big white box stuffed
with his high-end med school education,
he says: *Your diagnosis is unclear.*
I'm prescribing Paxil because
I can't really see you.
I say: *My diagnosis is pissed off,*
is can't-take-this-shit-anymore.
No, I don't want your goddamn prescription.

Jan Beatty
I Knew I Wasn't Poor

I knew I wasn't poor,
because I had a choice:
buy tampons or birth control pills.
I shoplifted.
When I opened the oven door,
splitting the closet-sized kitchen in half,
my only plan was heat.
The ice smooth on the inside of the windows,
the no money to pay the bill.
I knew I wasn't poor,
because I could always eat
at the restaurant where I waitressed.
I never went hungry.
I waited for the rich customer,
bored with her herb chicken—
to toss it: *No, I don't want to take it*
with me. We're going to the theater.
I secreted that half-plate of turned-
over food, and like a miser or explorer,
stashed it in my locker in the restaurant's
dark hallway. I had no shame, I was finding
my solution: how to eat, how to live,
I felt accomplishment. No insurance for
my beater car, I threw parking tickets in
the backseat with a flurry. I grew rich in
my imaginings. The People's Clinic when
I was too sick to last it out. I knew I wasn't poor,
and when my clothes wore raggedy and
I got angry at what I couldn't have, I walked
into the department store with an empty bag,
filling my heart, filling the holes
that were everywhere.

Tara Betts
Failed Spells

For almost four years, I lived in Rod Serling's hometown,
and the sun would disappear and stay gone, as if East
Seattle or lower Alaska claimed me. All the days circled
so mundane, drab as bus stops, but that quiet sounded
nothing like the hush after election day, almost as quiet
as pipeline contracts and murderers acquitted by mistrials
or paid leaves, death older than all. Remember we can't
drink oil, and oil makes money, but no one can eat that either,
even if pennies rest their tinny savor on tongues like blood.

The sidewalks of Washington Heights and Brooklyn feel
solid, too damned quiet before spray painted swastikas,
ripped hijabs, and burned churches can be tallied. What
can be said to the man with access to the button when he
is more concerned with tweets? He'd kill birds for a profit,
collateral damage. What country is this? The land where
company towns and segregation threaded the railroads
and cotton fields, but this same earth, this cursed and
blessed soil is where we say no. The fields where promises
of powerful fools will bow some, but promises are destined
to go brittle, break into failed spells that will be uttered again.

Richard Blanco
Dreaming a Wall

I would build a great wall, and nobody
builds walls better than me, believe me . . .
              —DONALD TRUMP

He hates his neighbors' flowers, claims his
are redder, bluer, whiter than theirs, believes
his bees work harder, his soil richer, blacker.
He hears birds sing sweeter in his trees, taller
and fuller, too, but not enough to screen out
the nameless faces next door that he calls
liars, thieves who'd steal his juicier fruit, kill
for his wetter rain and brighter sun. He keeps
a steely eye on them, mocks the too-cheery
colors of their homes, too small and too close
to his own, painted white, with room to spare.
He curses the giggles of their children always
barefoot in the yard, chasing their yappy dogs.
He wishes them dead. Closes his blinds. Refuses
to let light from their windows pollute his eyes
with their lives. Denies their silhouettes dining
at the kitchen table, laughing in the living room,
the goodnight kisses through every bedroom.
Slouched in his couch, grumbling over the news
he dismisses as fake, he changes the channel
to an old cowboy Western. Amid the clamor
of gunshots, he dozes off thinking of his dream
where he stakes a line between him and all
his neighbors, stabs the ground as he would
their chests. Forms a footing cast in blood-red
earth, bends steel bars as he would their bones
with his bare fists and buries them in concrete.
Mortar mixed thick with anger, each brick laid
heavy with revenge, he smiles as he finishes
the last course high enough to imagine them
more miserable and lonely than him alone
behind his wall, worshiping his greener lawn,
praising his fresher air, under his bluer sky.

Richard Blanco
Complaint of El Río Grande

for Aylin Barbieri

I was meant for all things to meet:
to make the clouds pause in the mirror
of my waters, to be home to fallen rain
that finds its way to me, to turn eons
of loveless rock into lovesick pebbles
and carry them as humble gifts back
to the sea which brings life back to me.

I felt the sun flare, praised each star
flocked about the moon long before
you did. I've breathed air you'll never
breathe, listened to songbirds before
you could speak their names, before
you dug your oars in me, before you
created the gods that created you.

Then countries—your invention—maps
jigsawing the world into colored shapes
caged in bold lines to say: you're here,
not there, you're this, not that, to say:
yellow isn't red, red isn't black, black is
not white, to say: *mine*, not *ours*, to say
war, and believe life's worth is relative.

You named me big river, drew me—blue,
thick to divide, to say: *spic* and *Yankee*,
to say: *wetback* and *gringo*. You split me
in two—half of me *us*, the rest *them*. But
I wasn't meant to drown children, hear
mothers' cries, never meant to be your
geography: a line, a border, or murderer.

I was meant for all things to meet:
the mirrored clouds and sun's tingle,
birdsongs and the quiet moon, the wind

and its dust, the rush of mountain rain—
and us. Blood that runs in you is water
flowing in me, both life, the truth we
know we know: be one in one another.

Rafael Campo
From Ten Patients and Another

II. Jamal

The patient is a three-year-old black male,
The full-term product of a pregnancy
That was, according to his grandmother,
Unplanned and maybe complicated by
Prenatal alcohol exposure. Did
OK, developmentally delayed
But normal weights and heights, until last week
When he ingested what's turned out to be
Cocaine, according to the lab results;
His grandmother had said she'd seen him with
Some baby powder on his face and hands
Before he started seizing and they brought
Him in. The vital signs have stabilized.
The nurse is getting DSS involved.
The mom? She left it on the kitchen table.
That's her—the one who sings to him all night.

IV. Kelly

The patient is a twelve-year-old white female.
She's gravida zero, no STD's.
She'd never even had a pelvic. One
Month nausea and vomiting. No change
In bowel habits. No fever, chills, malaise.
Her school performance has been worsening.
She states that things at home are fine.
On physical exam, she cried but was
Cooperative. Her abdomen was soft,
With normal bowel sounds and question of
A suprapubic mass, which was non-tender.
Her pelvic was remarkable for scars
At six o'clock, no hymen visible,
Some uterine enlargement. Pregnancy
Tests positive times two. She says it was
Her dad. He's sitting in the waiting room.

VII. Manuel

In Trauma 1, a gay Latino kid—
I think he's seventeen—is getting tubed
For respiratory failure. "Sleeping pills
And Tylenol," I translated for him
As he was wheeled in. His novio
Explained that when he'd told his folks about
It all, they threw him out. Like trash. They lived
Together underneath the overpass
Of Highway 101 for seven weeks,
The stars obstructed from their view. For cash,
They sucked off older men in Cadillacs;
A viejita from the neighborhood
Brought tacos to them secretly. Last night,
With eighteen-wheelers roaring overhead,
He whispered that he'd lost the will to live.
He pawned his crucifix to get the pills.

XI. Jane Doe #2

They found her unresponsive in the street
Beneath a lamplight I imagined made
Her seem angelic, regal even, clean.
She must have been around sixteen. She died
Who knows how many hours earlier
That day, the heroin inside her like
A vengeful dream about to be fulfilled.
Her hands were crossed about her chest, as though
Raised up in self-defense; I tried to pry
Them open to confirm the absence of
A heartbeat, but in death she was so strong,
As resolute as she was beautiful.
I traced the track marks on her arms instead,
Then pressed my thumb against her bloodless lips,
So urgent was my need to know. I felt
The quiet left by a departing soul.

Rafael Campo
The Chart

Says fifty-four-year-old obese Hispanic
female—I wonder if they mean the one
with long black braids, Peruvian, who sells
tamales at the farmer's market, tells
me I'm too thin, I better eat; or is
she the Dominican with too much rouge
and almond eyes at the dry cleaners who
must have been beautiful in her youth;
or maybe she's the Cuban lady drunk
on grief who I've seen half-asleep, alone
as if that bench were only hers, the park
her home at last; or else the Mexican
who hoards the littered papers she collects
and says they are her "documents"; if not,
it could be the Colombian drug addict
whose Spanish, even when she's high, is perfect;
or maybe it's the one who never says
exactly where she's from, but who reminds
me of my grandmother, poor but refined,
lace handkerchief balled up in her plump hand,
who died too young from a condition that
some doctor, nose in her chart, overlooked.

Rafael Campo
The Good Doctor

A doctor lived in a city
Full of dying men and women.
He ministered to them
A medicine admittedly

Not curative, and only
Slightly toxic. The medicine
Was known as empathy. It worked
Until the doctor grew more lonely—

His patients only died less quickly—
And in a fit of rage
He burned its formula.
Word spread to the sickly

As the virus had: precise
And red, omitting nothing.
The doctor's reputation changed.
No longer was he viewed as wise;

Instead, when patients came
To him they brought suspicion;
They held their breath when he would try
To hear their songs. His names,

Once various and musical,
Were soon forgotten.
When he died of the disease,
They left him where he fell.

Cyrus Cassells
The World That the Shooter Left Us

In this one, ladies and gentlemen,
Beware, be clear: the brown man,

The able lawyer, the paterfamilias,
Never makes it out of the poem alive:

The rash, all-too-daily report,
The out-of-the-blue bullet

Blithely shatters our treasured
Legal eagle's bones and flesh—

In the brusque spectacle of point-blank force,
On a crimsoned street,

Where a revered immigrant plummets
Over a contested parking spot,

And the far-seeing sages insist,
Amid strident maenads

Of at-the-ready patrol car sirens,
Clockwork salvos,

The charismatic Latino lawyer's soul
Is banished, elsewhere, without a shred

Of eloquence in the matter—
And the brute, churning

Surfaces of the world,
They bear our beloved citizen away—

Which means, austere saints
And all-seeing masters,

If I grasp your bracing challenge:
At our lives' most brackish hour,

Our highest mission isn't just to bawl,
But to turn the soul-shaking planet

Of the desecrated parking lot
(The anti-miracle),

The blunt, irascible white man's
Unnecessary weapon,

And the ruse of self-defense
Into justice-cries and ballots?

Into newfound pledges and particles of light?

in memory of J. Garza, 1949–2017

Hayan Charara
The Problem with Me Is the Problem with You

A dog outside is barking loudly. Inside, everything is quiet.
I said I would not, but here I am looking.

Dogs snarling and lunging at men naked and hooded.
Animals don't know shame, and mine I love

but not so much because love like oil spreads thin and clings—
to the heart, the mind, I don't know—

and I suspect she gets depressed when I leave her for days on end.
No woman has ever watched me close the door with such sad eyes.

Yes, I've changed the subject. Driving to the airport
I think these days people long for what is happening to make sense

or to make sense of what is happening: for example, the woman
holding the leash is smiling while the man attached to it

tries to hide his shame. Sometimes, men want to be like nature.
Speaking of which, all around hanging, falling, falling to pieces

the leaves of oak, pine, maple, magnolia, and cypress—
too many to count. I tell myself, there will be leaves to bag

when I return home, and, yes, it's a cliché to think this
and then think of men sent home in plastic bags.

Days like today, times like these, I don't want a damn thing
to do with victims. In the terminal, through the windows,

the twilight almost imperceptible, evening coming on quickly,
and the color of the sky I don't notice.

Waiting, I look around. Nothing here compares to anything there.
I may look like them, but I am not.

On the long flight I take the aisle for comfort, and the illusion
of safety, and I leave the view to the woman beside me

watching me—she looks like someone I would make small talk for,
buy a drink—and I speak kindly, an act like the weather,

as much prophecy as science, and like the weather
what makes me frightening—terror in her heart, her mind—

is invisible, capable of being identified or anticipated
only by those in the know. She has big brown eyes and I believe

that she believes at my mercy she will thrive or perish.
I reduce myself to clichés: talk about the weather.

When she says nothing at all, I think she is like everyone else,
myself included—an expert of sorts:

everyone knows something about someone.
And the wise are interpreters for those who cannot read the signs:

turbulence ahead, trouble to come, and on every horizon,
a disappearance.

Chen Chen
The School of Logic

I love you your Cheez-It-
      stained mouth. I love you
your legs, two furry examples
      of eternity. I love you your love
of instruction manuals, original
      packaging, the step-by-*Don't*
throw it out, don't you want to know
      how it works? I love you your logic,
your *Try it.* Your reaching
      for my hand again
in the South Plains Mall, Lubbock.
      Your flirty eyes in this A/C oasis
of mostly shoe stores.
      I don't love my refusing
to reach back.
      My logic of what if they spit, what if
fists. How I see
      every look. & think
we're too much love,
      even like, trying on shoes
side by side.
      How I can try on these clearly
gay sneakers, yet still leave
      A Buffer
between where I sit
      & you. How I've read
& never thrown out these instructions,
      their love
for telling me, *Under there, under*
      that under, that's where your family
         can see you.
But how I love you
      your seeing. Your grinning
Hey. Your soft *Come on,*
      hold my hand as we pass
the kiosk of aggressive
      T-shirt peddlers, the squawking

crew of college boys.
      Your *It's alright.*
Your *I'm here.* Your
      Fuck it & quick grip & before I
know it. Your logic
      more beautiful than mine.

Chen Chen
The School of Morning & Letters

Assigned to flurries
of dust, assigned to the dead
middle of winter in West Texas,

assigned to give assignments
in a building called English,
I walk to campus, rubbing flecks

of night from my eyes.
On my phone, the morning
headlines spell crisis,

the morning is picture
after picture of the coiffed like
cotton candy doom,

the chalky delirious face
of our leader, endorsed
by the KKK.

Assigned him, assigned
this season of k's & hard c's,
I look up & see the dark

birds called grackle,
congregating near English.
I catch, am caught in the winged

weather above food court & student
union. I listen to the grackle
orchestra of unrelenting

shriek. I study the blur
of their long-tailed swerving, their
bodies like comets, frenzied

commas, yet unable, finally,
to mark, to contain
the wide blue Texas sky.

Still, they try. Every beak
& claw, every uncalm feather
tries, as if the sky

were the only fact left,
as if the grackles
have been told to memorize it,

as if someone, someday,
will ask them to
speak it, this long blue sentence.

The guy who stole my girlfriend
in 1983 drove a rusted-out Beetle
and carried a .22 pistol for runs to the bank
to drop off nightly deposits from the General
Cinema, where he was Assistant Manager
and where I worked and saw *Rocky Horror*
about 20 times more than I wanted to
in egg-and-tp-drenched midnight shows.
He lived in a rat-trap, roach-infested, leaning-over
shack on the edge of The Heights,
a few streets over from the house where,
in 2004, a local TV reporter was murdered
in her bed, her face beaten beyond recognition.

*

In 1988, on my first night as Assistant Manager
at a restaurant in Dallas, a fight broke out
between a pimp and a private investigator,
who may also have been a pimp. A group
of frat boys decided to jump in and knocked
the whole scrum over onto the floor
just on the other side of the bar from me.
The pimp came up pointing a .22 semiautomatic
directly at the closest object, which happened
to be my forehead. He didn't shoot—
just waved his gun around until everyone
cowered under their tables—then
calmly walked out the front door and down the street.

*

My best friend in sixth or seventh grade
moved to Arkansas from New Mexico.
Ron's skin was lizard-rough.
He raised hamsters and hermit crabs.
I struck him out for the last out of the Little League

Championship. We went out to his father's farm
and shot cans and bottles with his .22 rifle.
Back in New Mexico, he'd had some health problems
and his mother had shot herself in the head.
A few years ago, a dead body was found
buried on his father's property. Ron's son
ended up shooting himself in the head as well.
He was 22.

*

On December 14, 2012, an armed intruder
entered the Sandy Hook School with a pistol,
a .223 Bushmaster, hundreds of rounds of ammunition,
and a shotgun in the car. Rather than turn right,
toward my wife's classroom where she pulled
two kids into her room from the hallway,
he turned to the left, murdered twenty children
and six adults, including the principal
and the school psychologist, both of whom
went into the hallway to stop the gunman,
and shot two other teachers, who survived.
After that, a lot of other things happened,
but it doesn't really matter what.

Brian Clements
Grievance

It used to be that one wrapped oneself in a sentence about birds
And walked out into an orchard or floated among the mangroves
Confident that, should no bird be there nor anyone to hear,
The words themselves would suffice to bear
The little marvels of the mundane into their spotlights
Among the newsday chaos. It used to be that beauty resided
In whatever stepped into the foreground, composed itself
Sufficiently to stand out against and amidst the background static
And sing directly to a neural path, that a moment of clarity
Might bloom from the mess of theory like a parakeet
Come to rest on your knee during a business lunch. But these days
It seems irresponsible not to face up to everything
Wrong, to write *birds* or *orchards* or *mangroves*
Without writing the death of the bees, the immortality
Of slave trade, of plastic flotillas roaming the Pacific,
Or crude oil coating the floor of the Gulf.
It used to be that a word would flutter through the window,
Maybe two or three more would follow, and, suddenly,
Birds. But now every window is destined for bulletproofing,
Every classroom, well, who wants to hear about that?
All anyone wants anymore are jokes and memes and TV
Versions of their own lives in high def. I know that isn't true,
But it used to be that I wasn't the least bit concerned about who
Was listening; I just hoped to pour a poultice into your ear
That would make you hum.
Now all I want is to pull up a chair,
To sit down facing each other, and tell you
What happened and where it hurts.

Jim Daniels
Crack the Whip

Endless downpour had splattered
the campground into gray mud.
We bought rawhide whips
at the pseudo-Indian tourist
shop in Muskegon. Our bleary father
paid, wanting only to be beery,
his vacation washing away. Leaky
tent, wet matches, droopy cigarettes.

Perhaps that explains my brother
crafting a lethal tomahawk
for my son on a rainy vacation
35 years later. My wife flung it
in the lake where it sunk
with a plunk as my brother
and son both cried out.

In the basement back home,
we cracked those whips to hear
whose echoed loudest. We strutted
city sidewalks, flicking wildly at trees,
bushes, cats, dogs, and younger children.
It hurt. We knew it hurt.

The store offered no Indian explanation
for the whips, nor the display case
of switchblades and stilettos
imported from Mexico, illegal except
in that square mile of local politics.

The whips hung on hooks
near our mother scrubbing laundry
under a crucifix dangling above washtubs.
The old saints whipped themselves
for God. Jesus, sweet Jesus.

The cheap dyed feathers of my headdress
fell out in the car when my father reached back
to smack somebody. At home, our streets ran
long and straight. Our whips curled
into frayed snakes, live wires sparking.

Nothing is simple. I apologize for suggesting
otherwise. Eyes watered with pain.
Apologies never enough. Whip—
—lash! Gnashing sound bitten off.

Those whips could still be landing
on somebody. My mother prayed
to merciful Jesus while my father swore
in the name of God the Father, the cruel one.

The cracked whip of our laughter
at the howls of pain. You can only
crack a whip at the air so many times.
Trust me. Or, better yet, don't.
Throw the tomahawk in the lake.

Jim Daniels
My Two Aunts

work at Burger King and McDonald's.
One in Newark, the other in Memphis.
My two aunts married two drunks—
one died, the other disappeared.

My two aunts are two alcoholics,
recovering. One dates a blind man.
The other dates memory:
her husband's final day
breathing his own blood.

Their alcoholic sons
have married and divorced.
Their children are sad and overweight
they are tall and stutter
they have imaginary illnesses
they blame their fathers
they blame their mothers
they smoke one endless cigarette.

But my two aunts,
they are saying *May I help you?*
and *Big Mac and fries?*
and *Whopper and fries?*
They are amazed by and resigned to
the goofy hats and polyester slacks.

They take orders from bosses
younger than their children.
They pledge allegiance to the burger corp.
After work they put their feet up
and reach for the imaginary drink.

One lost the condo paying off
shared credit cards after the divorce.
The other lost the house after the husband
lost his salesman's job after 27 years,

lost his factory job after six months,
ended up a janitor swigging wine
in a broom closet.

My two aunts take off their sour uniforms
and sleep or don't sleep, depending.
Big Mac and a Quarter Pounder.
Whopper. Itchy collar, swollen feet.

No more Cheerios for dinner
no more shakes and instant regrets
no more half-gallon-vodka guilt and lies.
One aunt bites holes in her lips
and takes community college classes in math.
The other started aerobics
with matching leotard and sweat band.

It's a matter of time,
they both say, *I'm getting on*
my feet again. AA, the church.
Belief, addiction,
addiction, belief.
May I help you please?
Please, may I help you?

One aunt wants her marriage
annulled: they were teenagers and not
in their right mind for thirty years.
The other says she's stopped visiting
the grave but hasn't.

My two aunts are getting
their lives together.
They have shed their soggy dreams
they are selling hamburgers
in America for minimum wage
they are trying to shed
their scales and bad news.

If only they could give up
on bad news, swear it off.
What put them here

pressing buttons, handing out change?
Thank you, yes, thank you.
Here is your order.

My two aunts smoke now,
more than they ever drank.
My two aunts, one way or another
we will kill them.

Kwame Dawes
On Hearing News of Another Shot Black Man

I am in the lemon-green room. This room
as if the color has exploded the softening
comfort of green, covering the worn
books, the discarded folders—let me say
that this is a green of the shade of light
filtering through leaves—imagine a bowl
of green olives or grapes in their variety
of shades, this is the green I speak of,
and I must be clear about this, for green
is as fickle as the bodies we live in—this
green has exploded over the room and settled
gently over the reams of paper, the boxes
in the multivoiced shades of my island.
And I sit here, dappled as if the trees
above are the filter over me
and that lime tree, stunted by acid
in the root, in the corner smiles
sheepishly—I am here thinking
of the sensuality of the dye that covers
us and turns us into creatures
longing for shadows or startling
light, because I am feeling the news,
the news of a body broken by bullets,
by the illogic of why, by sorrows—
forgive me for asking you to take
me into your verdant back room,
forgive me if I sit quietly in the corner
rocking, maybe, but hoping for earth
to hold my vegetable self steady.

Kwame Dawes
Capitalism

Soon the people forgot everything—
the women saw his pouting lips
and caught the sweetmeats that fell
from them and imagined them jewels.

If you squat and shit out rubies,
opals, and onyx stones, this magic
will turn your asshole into a relic
of faith. This is all an illusion
of course, but people have dreamed
of less and lived in joy for months.

Every battered person knows
that their greatest guilt and shame
is the emptiness they feel when
the beating stops. This too
is an illusion, but the little boy sold
his cows for a handful of colored
beans and he ran home rejoicing.

The two women on the canvas
are forgetting their nakedness
because they are forever in repose—
and the truest art lies in the muddy
palette that made them. All delusions.

The despot has given us the language
of relief. He smiles and says *heart*
as a doctor would say to you, *Your heart, sir.*

Where is the monster we imagined?
Lurking in the shadows. Look closely
into the brown gloom behind the woman!
He is there, this is the truth, well-dressed

and gloating. Soon the people forget
what is coming; it is the art of silence.

The despot feeds on the lull
in the air, he grows fat.

Chard deNiord
Checklist

the bone that aches in the rain of lies

a turnip instead of cake

the fire that feeds on the breath of witnesses, even a stone, then speaks

the echo of her no in the outskirts and streets

the sword he brought instead of peace

the red coal an angel places on the tongue like a treat

the sentence of *his* sentence

pennies worth more than gold

others, and then some

the tree with so many tongues that says,
"The truth resides inside the wind and blows
for those who hear it."

a kiss on the cheek that doesn't turn

the nerve that takes its stand by keeping its seat

the pauper in the park who says,
"Of these ends, it is the Right of the People to alter or abolish it."

the bell that heals itself by ringing

a smile in the hole

the eye that sees when closed

waking, waking

Dante Di Stefano
American Dream, 2018

Even the unsaid words on our neighbors' lips
sound like murder more often than they should;
the cherry blossoms withhold their riots
on the edge of my sleep most evenings now.
No, that's not quite right. I'm afraid of likes,
bombs, apps, drone strikes, swipes and hashtags, agents
of the state, pandemics, bans, placebos.
What I mean to say is: I am afraid
of arsenals, electorates, committees,
the touchscreen, the cankered art of the deal.
I am waiting for the charge, for the fuse,
for the final detonation, for time
and the stars and the smell of fresh cut grass
wafting through suburbs to cease and desist.

Dante Di Stefano
Cradle Song

for Luciana, one month old

One squall from your tiny body, fevered
in the night, outweighs an electorate,
undoes the disgust that knots up my throat
with talk of Power and its Founding Fathers.

You're not the first to come into a world
where bad men bleed the meek, lie about it,
and smile. Burrow deeper into my shirt,
arching bluebell of my most hopeful hour.

For far too few years I know you'll be safe
in our home, but after that your nation
will try to teach you its collateral
vocabularies of shackle and pledge.

Don't learn them. Your birthright is no baton.
Don't wield it. Beacon it, this broken hymn,
this lullaby your father sings for you,
made of spindrift love and rage and larkspur.

Kathy Engel
Now I Pray

Ashen face, wool hat bobbing,
the young boy's eyes dart to me,
then up at the man pulling a rolling
suitcase, whose hand he holds,
then back at me. His legs move
as if without gravity. The man asks:
Do you know a church on this street
that serves free food? I want to say
I know. That the names of churches
on an Avenue called Americas roll
out of me. I want to tell you
it is temporary, their condition:
suitcase, darting eyes, seeking free
food at 9 p.m. in a big city on a school night.
I want to tell you I don't for a moment
wonder if that is really the boy's father
or uncle or legitimate caretaker—
something in the handholding and
eyes, having watched too many
episodes of *Law and Order*. I want
to tell you I take them to a restaurant
and pay for a warm meal or empty
my wallet not worrying how
offensive that might be because
in the end hunger is hunger.
I want to tell you I call someone
who loves them—that there is someone—
and say your guys are lost, can
you come? I want to tell you I sit
down on the sidewalk at the corner
of Waverly and pray—that all
passing by, anonymous shoes
marking the pavement, join
in a chorus of prayer humming
like cicadas in the Delta. I want to

tell you the boy and the man eat food
encircled by the warmth of bodies.
I want to turn the cold night into a feast.
I will tell you I am praying.

Martín Espada
Letter to My Father

October 2017

You once said: *My reward for this life will be a thousand pounds of dirt
shoveled in my face.* You were wrong. You are seven pounds of ashes
in a box, a Puerto Rican flag wrapped around you, next to a red brick
from the house in Utuado where you were born, all crammed together
on my bookshelf. You taught me there is no God, no life after this life,
so I know you are not watching me type this letter over my shoulder.

When I was a boy, you were God. I watched from the seventh floor
of the projects as you walked down into the street to stop a public
execution: a big man caught a small man stealing his car, and everyone
in Brooklyn heard the car alarm wail of the condemned: *He's killing me.*
At a word from you, the executioner's hand slipped from the hair
of the thief. *The kid was high*, was all you said when you came back to us.

When I was a boy, and you were God, we flew to Puerto Rico. You said:
My grandfather was the mayor of Utuado. His name was Buenaventura.
That means good fortune. I believed in your grandfather's name.
I heard the tree frogs chanting to each other all night. I saw banana
leaf and elephant palm sprouting from the mountain's belly. I gnawed
the mango's pit, and the sweet yellow hair stuck between my teeth.
I said to you: *You came from another planet. How did you do it?*
You said: *Every morning, just before I woke up, I saw the mountains.*

Every morning, I see the mountains. In Utuado, three sisters,
all in their seventies, all bedridden, all Pentecostales who only left
the house for church, lay sleeping on mattresses spread across the floor
when the hurricane gutted the mountain the way a butcher slices open
a dangled pig, and a rolling wall of mud buried them, leaving the fourth
sister to stagger into the street, screaming like an unheeded prophet
about the end of the world. In Utuado, a man who cultivated a garden
of aguacate and carambola, feeding the avocado and star fruit to his
nieces from New York, saw the trees in his garden beheaded all at once
like the soldiers of a beaten army, and so hanged himself. In Utuado,
a welder and a handyman rigged a pulley with a shopping cart to ferry

rice and beans across the river where the bridge collapsed, witnessed
the cart swaying above so many hands, then raised a sign that told
the helicopters: *Campamento los Olvidados: Camp of the Forgotten.*

Los olvidados wait seven hours in line for a government meal of Skittles
and Vienna sausage, or a tarp to cover the bones of a house with no roof,
as the fungus grows on their skin from sleeping on mattresses drenched
with the spit of the hurricane. They drink the brown water, waiting
for microscopic monsters in their bellies to visit plagues upon them.
A nurse says: *These people are going to have an epidemic. These people
are going to die.* The president flips rolls of paper towels to a crowd
at a church in Guaynabo, Zeus lobbing thunderbolts on the locked ward
of his delusions. Down the block, cousin Ricardo, Bernice's boy, says
that somebody stole his can of diesel. I heard somebody ask you once
what Puerto Rico needed to be free. And you said: *Tres pulgadas
de sangre en la calle: Three inches of blood in the street.* Now, three
inches of mud flow through the streets of Utuado, and troops patrol
the town, as if guarding the vein of copper in the ground, as if a shovel
digging graves in the backyard might strike the ore below, as if la brigada
swinging machetes to clear the road might remember the last uprising.

I know you are not God. I have the proof: seven pounds of ashes in a box
on my bookshelf. Gods do not die, and yet I want you to be God again.
Stride from the crowd to seize the president's arm before another roll
of paper towels sails away. Thunder Spanish obscenities in his face.
Banish him to a roofless rainstorm in Utuado, so he unravels, one soaked
sheet after another, till there is nothing left but his cardboard heart.

I promised myself I would stop talking to you, white box of grey grit.
You were deaf even before you died. Hear my promise now: I will take you
to the mountains, where houses lost like ships at sea rise blue and yellow
from the mud. I will open my hands. I will scatter your ashes in Utuado.

George Evans
Borderline

Thinking somebody might one day come to claim him,
the gravediggers left their rope around the coffin, illegal
themselves, living job to job, knowing what it means
to lose track of someone planted beneath the leaves,
and that bonds are not broken by borders, borders
are not bonds, and walls force things into secret.

They know that so far no laws created by men and women
reach into the grave, that death is not separate from living,
and that some are freer below ground than above,
bellies stuffed with drug balloons, fingers chopped off
from fieldwork, legs trembling from standing at conveyors
all day without food, scrubbing filth, making beds, or waiting
on corners for those who need their labor to show up in trucks
with shovels and picks to ferry them over death's next river.

George Evans
The Altar

She sleeps in the ICBC (Industrial and Commercial Bank of China) vestibule, north
corner of 20th Avenue and Noriega, converting it to a *retablo* every night she's there—
who drifts and roams—a bright altar facing the intersection catty-corner, one block east
of once another corner bank (now brokerage) with a bullet hole in the upper right corner
of its west-facing gold aluminum window frame, put there in 1974 by Patty Hearst after
robbing a once–Hibernia Bank next corner down, one block west (now health clinic)—
it can all be seen on Google Maps. "*Hearst—heart with a twisty S,*" she says fencing
herself in for the night with the train of suitcases and wheeled baskets she moves piece
by piece, inch by inch, corner to corner, mile by mile, every day, all day, shooed as a pest
door to door down to the ocean and back, exhausted, overweight yet endlessly hungry,
hesitant to beg but begging, ashamed to beg but begging, and, even with her stench, beard,
enormous weight, and hair plastered by years of weather, she's fearful of city shelter men
"*who'd even rape gopher holes,*" preferring doorways, bus stops, trees and bushes, lulled
by dreams of further, simpler worlds, "*Swept out to sea, embraced and gently rocked.*"

San Francisco

Tarfia Faizullah
Self-Portrait as Mango

She says, *Your English is great! How long have you been in our country?*
I say, *Suck on a mango, bitch, since that's all you think I eat anyway.* Mangoes

are what margins like me know everything about, right? Doesn't
a mango just win spelling bees and kiss white boys? Isn't a mango

a placeholder in a poem folded with burkas? But this one,
the one I'm going to slice and serve down her throat, is a mango

that remembers jungles jagged with insects, the river's darker thirst.
This mango was cut down by a scythe that beheads soldiers, mango

that taunts and suns itself into a hard-palmed fist only a few months
per year, fattens while blood stains green ponds. Why use a mango

to beat her perplexed? Why not a coconut? Because this "exotic" fruit
won't be cracked open to reveal whiteness to you. This mango

isn't alien just because of its gold-green bloodline. I know
I'm worth waiting for. I want to be kneaded for ripeness. Mango:

my own sunset-skinned heart waiting to be held and peeled, mango
I suck open with teeth. *Tappai!* This is the only way to eat a mango.

Carolyn Forché
The Boatman

We were thirty-one souls, he said, in the gray-sick of sea
in a cold rubber boat, rising and falling in our filth.
By morning this didn't matter, no land was in sight,
all were soaked to the bone, living and dead.
We could still float, we said, from war to war.
What lay behind us but ruins of stone piled on ruins of stone?
City called "mother of the poor" surrounded by fields
of cotton and millet, city of jewelers and cloak-makers,
with the oldest church in Christendom and the Sword of Allah.
If anyone remains there now, he assures, they would be utterly alone.
There is a hotel named for it in Rome two hundred meters
from the Piazza di Spagna, where you can have breakfast under
the portraits of film stars. There the staff cannot do enough for you.
But I am talking nonsense again, as I have since that night
we fetched a child, not ours, from the sea, drifting face
down in a life vest, its eyes taken by fish or the birds above us.
After that, Aleppo went up in smoke, and Raqqa came under a rain
of leaflets warning everyone to go. Leave, yes, but go where?
We lived through the Americans and Russians, through Americans
again, many nights of death from the clouds, mornings surprised
to be waking from the sleep of death, still unburied and alive
with no safe place. Leave, yes, we'll obey the leaflets, but go where?
To the sea to be eaten, to the shores of Europe to be caged?
To *camp misery* and *camp remain here*. I ask you then, where?
You tell me you are a poet. If so, our destination is the same.
I find myself now the boatman, driving a taxi at the end of the world.
I will see that you arrive safely, my friend, I will get you there.

Carolyn Forché
Mourning

A peacock on an olive branch looks beyond
the grove to the road, beyond the road to the sea,
blank-lit, where a sailboat anchors to a cove.
As it is morning, below deck a man is pouring water into a cup,
listening to the radio-talk of the ships: barges dead
in the calms awaiting port call, pleasure boats whose lights
hours ago went out, fishermen setting their nets for mullet,
as summer tavernas hang octopus to dry on their lines,
whisper smoke into wood ovens, sweep the terraces
clear of night, putting the music out with morning
light, and for the breath of an hour it is possible
to consider the waters of this sea *wine-dark*, to remember
that there was no word for blue among the ancients,
but there was the whirring sound before the oars
of the great triremes sang out of the seam of world,
through pine-sieved winds silvered by salt flats until
they were light enough to pass for breath from the heavens,
troubled enough to fell ships and darken thought—
then as now the clouds pass, roosters sleep in their huts,
the sea flattens under glass air, but there is nothing to hold us there:
not the quiet of marble nor the luff of sail, fields of thyme,
a vineyard at harvest, and the sea filled with the bones of those
in flight from wars east and south, our wars, their remains
scavenged on the sea floor and in its caves, belongings now
a flotsam washed to the rocks. Stand here and look
into the distant haze, there where the holy mountain
with its thousand monks wraps itself in shawls of rain,
then look to the west, where the rubber boats tipped
into the tough waves. Rest your eyes there, remembering the words
of Anacreon, himself a refugee of war, who appears
in the writings of Herodotus:
I love and do not love, I am mad and I am not mad.
For if the earth is a camp and the sea an ossuary of souls,
light your signal fires wherever you find yourselves.
Come the morning, launch your boats.

Denice Frohman
Puertopia

Puerto: port, from Latin "porta," meaning "gate, door";
Utopia: modern Latin meaning "nowhere"

the coquís don't sing anymore / they click / mosquitoes turned drones /
metropolis of crypto-bro / tax-deductible greed / a door opens / an island
drowns / a playground emerges / a boy / his toy // depending on the faith /
the most dangerous part of a wealthy man is his index finger / what he points to
/ who he lands on / a civilization disposable income / pirate in cargo shorts /
New World / Old Order // meanwhile / we diaspora / separated by sea / peel
plátanos & cut them on the same angle our mothers taught us to clap / when
the plane lands on either shore / now / the beaches are gated & no one knows
the names of the dead / now / investors clean their beaks in the river & this
is how a man becomes a flood // landlord of nothing / king of no good sky /
watch paradise / misbehave / watch the night pearl / into a necklace of fists
watch this / El Yunque / a real god machine / unhinge her jaw / & swallow
the flock / ¿where are the Puerto Ricans? / cuchifrito ghost town / battery-
operated citizenship / an island is not a tarmac / a disaster is not a destination—

Danielle Legros Georges
Poem for the Poorest Country in the Western Hemisphere

O poorest country, this is not your name.
You should be called beacon. You should

be called flame. Almond and bougainvillea,
garden and green mountain, villa and hut,

girl with red ribbons in her hair,
books under arm, charmed by the light

of morning, charcoal seller in black skirt,
encircled by dead trees. You, country,

are merchant woman and eager clerk,
grandfather at the gate, at the crossroads

with the flashlight, with all in sight.

Danielle Legros Georges
Shithole

eeeeeeeeeeeeeeeeeeeeeeeeeeeeeeeeeeeeee

I am the interrupter, hijacking your train
of thoughts. Call me maldito, cabrón,

La Bestia. Get on top of me and I'll throw
you off after you beg. I'll ride you like

a borrowed mule. Drive you across the river
and sell you up it. Call me coyote. Call me

wolf. Call me whatever the fuck animal
you like. Missionary. Priest. Call me

Mr. President. I'm all green. A blue gasp.
I'm the womb sterilizer, syringe and suction.

I'll drown you in a teaspoon of potassium
chloride. I was born an abomination.

At the age of one I crawled out of the Congo
dragging my sack full of hands.

At the age of two I mechanized my scythe.
At the age of three I wove myself a cape of flies.

At the age of four I blew the noses off
Sphinxes and studied the hieroglyphs

of your tomb. At the age of five I became
an angel, cunning, big-eared. At the age

of six I shot down the moon then I shot down
the sun. I am a nuclear bomb set for noon,

the paratext of your nightmare,
the translator of your tribulation.

I am a constipation. The worm nestled
in your colon. The parasite entering

your left ear. The sweetest liar. The drone
of your inner war. The architect of your gas

chamber. The poisoner of your water.
The multiplier. I am the radioactive

sphincter. The unthinkable, intolerable,
bleached ass.

Maria Mazziotti Gillan
Daddy, We Called You

"Daddy," we called you, "Daddy,"
when we talked to each other in the street,
pulling on our American faces,
shaping our lives in Paterson slang.

Inside our house, we spoke
a Southern Italian dialect
mixed with English
and we called you Papa

but outside again, you became Daddy
and we spoke of you to our friends
as "my father"
imagining we were speaking
of that *Father Knows Best*
TV character
in his dark business suit,
carrying his briefcase into his house,
retreating to his paneled den,
his big living room and dining room,
his frilly-aproned wife
who greeted him at the door
with a kiss. Such space

and silence in that house.
We lived in one big room—
living room, dining room, kitchen, bedroom,
all in one, dominated by the gray oak dining table
around which we sat, talking and laughing,
listening to your stories,
your political arguments with your friends.
Papa, how you glowed in company light,
happy when the other immigrants
came to you for help with their taxes
or legal papers.

It was only outside that glowing circle
that I denied you, denied your long hours
as night watchman in Royle Machine Shop.
One night, riding home from a date
my middle-class, American boyfriend
kissed me at the light; I looked up
and met your eyes as you stood at the corner

near Royle Machine. It was nearly midnight.
January. Cold and windy. You were waiting
for the bus, the street light illuminating
your face. I pretended I did not see you,
let my boyfriend pull away, leaving you
on the empty corner waiting for the bus
to take you home. You never mentioned it,
never said that you knew
how often I lied about what you did for a living
or that I was ashamed to have my boyfriend see you,
find out about your second-shift work, your broken English.

Today, remembering that moment,
still illuminated in my mind
by the streetlamp's gray light,
I think of my own son
and the distance between us
greater than miles.

Papa,
silk worker,
janitor,
night watchman,
immigrant Italian,
I honor the years you spent in menial work
slipping down the ladder
as your body failed you

while your mind, so quick and sharp,
longed to escape,
honor the times you got out of bed
after sleeping only an hour,
to take me to school or pick me up;

the warm bakery rolls you bought for me
on the way home from the night shift.

The letters
you wrote
to the editors
of local newspapers.

Papa,
silk worker,
janitor,
night watchman,
immigrant Italian,
better than any *Father Knows Best* father,
bland as white rice,
with your wine press in the cellar,
with the newspapers you collected
out of garbage piles to turn into money
you banked for us,
with your mouse traps,
with your cracked and calloused hands,
with your yellow teeth.
Papa,
dragging your dead leg
through the factories of Paterson,
I am outside the house now,
shouting your name.

Maria Mazziotti Gillan
I Want to Write a Poem to Celebrate

my father's arms, bulging and straining while he carries
the wooden box of dark purple grapes down the crumbling,
uneven cement steps into the cellar of the old house
on 19th street. The cellar, whitewashed by my mother,
grows darker as my father lumbers past the big coal
furnace and into the windowless wine room
at the very back where he will feed the grapes,
ripe and perfect and smelling of earth,
into the wine press. The grape smell changes
as they are crushed and drawn out into the fat
wooden barrels, and for weeks the cellar
will be full to the brim with the sweet smell
of grapes fermenting into wine, a smell I recognize
even forty years later each time I uncork a bottle,
an aroma that brings back my father
and his friends gathering under Zio Gianni's
grape arbor to play briscole through long July
nights, small glasses before them, peach slices
gleaming like amber in the ruby wine.

Aracelis Girmay
You Are Who I Love

January 20, 2017

You, selling roses out of a silver grocery cart

You, in the park, feeding the pigeons
You cheering for the bees

You with cats in your voice in the morning, feeding cats

You protecting the river.   You are who I love
delivering babies, nursing the sick

You with henna on your feet and a gold star in your nose

You taking your medicine, reading the magazines

You looking into the faces of young people as they pass, smiling and saying,
Alright! which, they know it, means *I see you, Family. I love you. Keep on.*

You dancing in the kitchen, on the sidewalk, in the subway waiting for the
train because Stevie Wonder, Héctor Lavoe, La Lupe

You stirring the pot of beans, you, washing your father's feet

You are who I love, you
reciting Darwish, then June

Feeding your heart, teaching your parents how to do The Dougie, counting to
10, reading your patients' charts

You are who I love, changing policies, standing in line for water, stocking the
food pantries, making a meal
You are who I love, writing letters, calling the senators, you who, with the
seconds of your body (with your *time* here), arrive on buses, on trains, in
cars, by foot to stand in the January streets against the cool and brutal offices,
saying: YOUR CRUELTY DOES NOT SPEAK FOR ME

You are who I love, you struggling to see
You struggling to love or find a question

You better than me, you kinder and so blistering with anger, you are who I love, standing in the wind, salvaging the umbrellas, graduating from school, wearing holes in your shoes

You are who I love
weeping or touching the faces of the weeping

You, Violeta Parra, grateful for the alphabet, for sound, singing toward us in the dream

You carrying your brother home
You noticing the butterflies

Sharing your water, sharing your potatoes and greens

You who did and did not survive
You who cleaned the kitchens
You who built the railroad tracks and roads
You who replanted the trees, listening to the work of squirrels and birds, you are who I love
You whose blood was taken, whose hands and lives were taken, with or without your saying
Yes, I mean to give. You are who I love.

You who the borders crossed
You whose fires
You decent with rage, so in love with the earth
You writing poems alongside children

You cactus, water, sparrow, crow   You, my elder
You are who I love,
summoning the courage, making the cobbler,

getting the blood drawn, sharing the difficult news, you always planting the marigolds, learning to walk wherever you are, learning to read wherever you are, you baking the bread, you come to me in dreams, you kissing the faces of your dead wherever you are, speaking to your children in your mother's languages, tootsing the birds

You are who I love, behind the library desk, leaving who might kill you, crying with the love songs, polishing your shoes, lighting the candles, getting through the first day despite the whisperers sniping fail fail fail

You are who I love, you who beat and did not beat the odds, you who knows that any good thing you have is the result of someone else's sacrifice, work, you who fights for reparations

You are who I love, you who stands at the courthouse with the sign that reads NO JUSTICE, NO PEACE

You are who I love, singing Leonard Cohen to the snow, you with glitter on your face, wearing a kilt and violet lipstick

You are who I love, sighing in your sleep

You, playing drums in the procession, you feeding the chickens and humming as you hem the skirt, you sharpening the pencil, you writing the poem about the loneliness of the astronaut

You wanting to listen, you trying to be so still

You are who I love, mothering the dogs, standing with horses

You in brightness and in darkness, throwing your head back as you laugh, kissing your hand
You carrying the berbere from the mill, and the jug of oil pressed from the olives of the trees you belong to

You studying stars, you are who I love
braiding your child's hair

You are who I love, crossing the desert and trying to cross the desert

You are who I love, working the shifts to buy books, rice, tomatoes, bathing your children as you listen to the lecture, heating the kitchen with the oven, up early, up late

You are who I love, learning English, learning Spanish, drawing flowers on your hand with a ballpoint pen, taking the bus home

You are who I love, speaking plainly about your pain, sucking your teeth at the airport terminal television every time the politicians say something that offends your sense of decency, of thought, which is often

You are who I love, throwing your hands up in agony or disbelief, shaking your head, arguing back, out loud or inside of yourself, holding close your incredulity which, yes, too, I love   I love

your working heart, how each of its gestures, tiny or big, stand beside my own agony, building a forest there

How "Fuck you" becomes a love song

You are who I love, carrying the signs, packing the lunches, with the rain on your face

You at the edges and shores, in the rooms of quiet, in the rooms of shouting, in the airport terminal, at the bus depot saying "No!" and each of us looking out from the gorgeous unlikelihood of our lives at all, finding ourselves here, witnesses to each other's tenderness, which, this moment, is fury, is rage, which, this moment, is another way of saying: *You are who I love   You are who I love   You and you and you are who*

Ruth Goring
The Hands That Wanted

November 8, 2016

It was the boil, the freeze,
the shutting of doors.
The day flapped like a filthy banner
on the line of our lives.
It swung and tied knots.
It was the freeze, the gray,
the eruption of infection.

The day opened and closed its mouth
again and again.
We were in some kind of current,
our cities like warships.
The smothering farmland,
innocent forests.
It was the boil, the day
flapped in helplessness,
the casual violation,
the people's terrified snarl.

We all wanted a blooming field,
a shelter. It was the failure,
the bricked up, the slammed.
We wanted a target,
we boiled and froze,
we thought we were choosing
but it was the familiar net
tightening in its familiar way
and some of us were comforted.

Adam Grabowski
The Plan

I'm bulletproof, nothing to lose
fire away, fire away.
—DAVID GUETTA, "Titanium," featuring Sia

I want to be bulletproof, she says,
from the back of the car, Ingrid, my daughter,
in the third grade.

Bulletproof, you want to be bulletproof,
like the song? I say into the rearview mirror.

Like a bulletproof vest, she says,
for school, I don't want to die.

This is what pop music has done to me,
7:50 A.M., this Wednesday ride to Sullivan Elementary.

She doesn't like the news
that filters out of our bedroom television
like an argument through a heating duct.

She doesn't like the regularity
of the drills now or the determination
in her teacher's voice, either,

but it's the closet
where they practice hiding
that has her rattled.
She can't always get a spot in the back.
It's the ones up front whose legs stick out
and you can still see their toes;
it's the ones up front who die.

She has a plan.
She'll hide in the bathroom.
Stand up on the toilet

where they can't see her legs.
She'll keep quiet. She's golden.

I was told once that parenting
is about slowly losing control,
that I can't walk in front of them forever
setting their world to order,
that the buildings get bigger and the fields get wider.
And now she's nine, and she has a plan.

I can tell her *go get heartbroken.*
I know about heartbroken.
I can tell her *if you're drunk I'll carry you home.*
I've been drunk and been carried home.

I don't know what to do
when your Converse are still peeking out
and there's a gun in the room.

She has a plan and I want to add
that if she's near the gym
she can take the side door.
Run as fast as she can.

But I'm wrong.
Just look at the place.
You can't even go outside anymore.

Parenting is about slowly losing control
and today is the first time my daughter gets to say
you have no idea what you're talking about,

the first time I can't say to her *I know exactly what you mean*
and mean it.

My eyes soften.
I am slowly losing control.

When Sia sings she means *Freedom.*
What my daughter hears is *Survival.*

A hidden place for every pair of legs,
skin unpierceable in a pierceable world.

In five minutes she'll be in school;
five minutes and she'll be on her own.

torrin a. greathouse
On Confinement

I sit across the table from my partner
      in the atrium of the psychiatric holding facility

            our hands churched into our laps. We are not allowed
to touch. The air between us thick as Perspex.

                They tell me all the ways this place resembles a prison.

          : :

Everything a sterile white
      so clean it could almost disinfect
         a memory.

          : :

In 1787,
      Jeremy Bentham conceived of what would become
         the most common prison design:

      the Panopticon.

      Intended to control prisoners through the illusion
      that they are always under surveillance.

          : :

My partner tells their therapist
they are afraid of taking
their own life,

      that they balanced on a building's edge,
      & three officers escort them from the room.

          : :

The first cop who ever handcuffed me
                    [was my father]
left me bound
                    till my fingers blued.

On the days when I can't remember
        his face,
            he becomes the scent of
                                    vodka & zip ties
                    the sound of
                        cuffs & a bottle
                        petaling into blades.

                            : :

        At the booking office they remove my glasses
        & the guards blur into a procession
        of fathers.

                            : :

        I bring my partner clothes & pads
when the hospital decides to hold them longer,

        shove each shirt that could mark them
as queer back inside the closet & shut it [like a mouth].

                            : :

        The word *faggot* scrawls across
        the jail guard's lips like graffiti.

                            : :

When I visit my partner
    they insist on staying inside

        the sky above
            the patio cordoned
        off with chicken wire.

                            : :

74

I plead my sentence down
in exchange for: my face, my prints, my DNA
      & ten years probation.

When I see a cop, I fear
      even my breath
           criminal

        & when my therapist asks me
        if I'm suicidal
           I lie.

Perhaps
both are a kind
of surveillance.

                  : :

Tear gas floods the street,
    sharpens water to a blade
    hidden in the orbit of my eye.

    & just like this, a squad car
        remakes my sadness a weapon.

If my partner snaps cuffs
    around my wrists

      [& I asked for this]

have they also weaponized
my desire?

                  : :

A woman in the facility
tells my partner:
    I know what you are.
Says:
    Sinner.
Says:
    Anti-christ.

My partner goads her on,
babbles in false
                tongues & is confined
                        to their room for *safety*.

                            : :

Once, a cop dragged me
into an alley &
                        beat me like he knew
                        exactly *what I was*.

    What does it say if sometimes
                    when I ask my partner to hit me

        I expect his fist
tightened in their throat, his voice
                    bruising their tongue?

                            : :

I am arrested & placed
                    [in the men's jail]
in solitary confinement.

        They tell me this is *protective
            custody*. That they couldn't afford
                the lawsuit if I were killed. In this way
                    they tell me, I am a woman

            only when I am no longer
                            breathing.

                            : :

The origin of the word *prison*
is the Latin *prehendere*—to take.

        It follows, then,
        that to take your life is to prison
        the body beneath dirt.

: :

[Historically,
        suicide is a criminal act].

                            : :

Balanced on a building's edge, I imagine
some permutation of this moment

                where to fail at death
                would be a breach

                            of my probation.

                            : :

We both weep for the first time

                        upon release

when we see the sky.

                        Pale blue

sliced through

                        with a single helix

of razor wire & bordered

                        in sterile white.

Laurie Ann Guerrero
Ars Política: How to Make Art

an ode to the artists of San Antonio, Tejas

You must start small as our mothers were small,
our fathers, too, small.

In a pillowcase whip-stitched with roses
or in an old coffee can, collect your abuelos'

teeth; assure them you will not bury them
near the bones of the dog that froze

the winter that dogs froze.
Carry the teeth under your tongue.

Let them root there.
This is how you will learn to speak.

Be ready to cough up songs, corridos plucked first
by a revolutionary whose gun smoke you wear in your hair.

The songs will be new in your throat. We are always
beginning. We are always beginning again.

You cannot be afraid to unhinge the jaw—
let the sun blister your mouth. Know thirst.

Cast your own eyes from their sockets like a confettied April
that you will know the bloom and battle of flowers.

Let your ribs draw across the ribs of another: el canto del violín.
Let your fingers dance: el guitarrón.

Needle or pen, brushed oil, machete or drum, leather,
cilantro, stomp—be patient in the tooling,

the weaving of experience one hundred, five hundred,
ten thousand years to here: love-making in the cotton and nopal,

battle lines and color lines, birthing in the huts, in the casitas
under a grove of mesquite and huizache,

and, too, lynchings and genocide in the feathery strands
of our DNA that move our hands to do the work.

Trust your hands know the work
even if you do not know the work.

You do not speak for the dead.
The dead speak for you.

Laurie Ann Guerrero
Three Hundred Years before These, Three Hundred Years After

a manifesto in celebration of the tricentennial anniversary of a city defeated

I come to clean the headstones that bear my names.
There is no one else I wish to speak to when I walk

away from the stove where I cook for my children
the beans I ate when I was a child. Gonzales:

with each candle I light with my conqueror hand,
let me praise my warrior feet in my city that is your body

that is my body: when the child leaves it, let us not forget
how to love him: let not my San Antonio forget that it is

home. I am a home. My children are caught in their studies—
spread across the city, the country, and still, though mine

is not the only hand that will feed them, I cook their beans.
Martinez: let me wear the boot soles of every man

who walked here, in whatever color skin he was born into,
that when I walk, my milk may let in honor of his mother.

You are his mother. I am his mother. What are we to do
in times like these but remain steady? Guerrero: let me praise

this rain that carries in it the ashes of my grandfather,
that in its swell through these streets feeds the mesquite.

That I am mesquite. I only want to feed my children.
I only want to speak to my dead. Velasquez: when you left

the classroom, the churchyard, the factory, tight in your army
greens, and felt your finger numb against the trigger,

did you tether your soul to the wild rose, to the soul of a lover
who may or may not reach your heaven? When the fire fills the sky,

call me lover. I know you understand this: though others cannot
hear us, it is not because we aren't singing.

Cortez: Correct in me the honoring of gold in our city,
gold faces and gold names, and gold hair, and gold shields,

and gold texts, and reliquaries of gold holding golden rings,
and histories so gold we celebrate the longing for gold

as our birthright. I am, too, a fair-haired, gold-seeking god.
I know you hear me. Tejeda: Teach me to praise the battles

we have lost in the clinics, in the schools, in the fields,
in the voting booth, and at the dinner table.

That when I walk away with my children, I am still walking.
I must keep walking. Threadbare, my San Antonio—do not erase me.

German-green eyes of my Tejano father, white skin of my Tejana mother,
my Spanish names, my Mexican mouth, my native and beating heart—

San Antonio is a city, whole. I am a city, whole. Let my revolution be
to sing graveside, to whisper intention into bowls of beans, to dance

without fear or fight. San Antonio is made of language: mightiest
tongue, mightiest voice—let me let go that pride.

Donald Hall
A Prophecy of Amos

I will strike down wooden houses; I will burn aluminum
clapboard skin; I will strike down garages
where crimson Toyotas sleep side by side; I will explode
palaces of gold, silver, and alabaster: the summer
great house and its folly together. Where shopping malls
spread plywood and plaster out, and roadhouses
serve steak and potato skins beside Alaska King Crab;
where triangular flags proclaim tribes of identical campers;
where airplanes nose to tail exhale kerosene,
weeds and ashes will drowse in continual twilight.

I reject the old house and the new car; I reject
Tory and Whig together; I reject the argument
that modesty of ambition is sensible because the bigger
they are the harder they fall; I reject Waterford;
I reject the five and dime; I reject Romulus and Remus;
I reject Martha's Vineyard and the slam dunk contest;
I reject leaded panes; I reject the appointment
made at the tennis net or on the seventeenth green;
I reject the Professional Bowling Tour;
I reject purple bathrooms with purple soap in them.

Men who lie awake worrying about taxes, vomiting
at dawn, whose hands shake as they administer Valium,
skin will peel from the meat of their thighs.
Armies that march all day with elephants past pyramids
and roll pulling missiles past Generals weary of saluting
and past President-Emperors splendid in cloth-of-gold,
rain will dissipate soft rumps of armies. Where square miles
of corn waver above Minnesota plains, where tobacco ripens
in Carolina and apples in New Hampshire, where soybeans
turn Kansas green, where pulp mills stink in Oregon,

dust will blow in the darkness and cactus die
before it flowers. Where skiers wait for chairlifts
wearing money, low raspberries will part rib bones.
Where the drive-in church raises a chromium cross,

dandelions and milkweed will straggle through blacktop.
I will strike from the ocean with waves afire;
I will strike from the hill with rain clouds of lava;
I will strike from darkened air

with melanoma in the shape of decorative hexagonals.
I will strike down embezzlers and eaters of snails.

Sam Hamill
Another Year

A huge yellow moon
rises above the great white mountain
on New Year's Eve.

It is nearly midnight.
I am sitting, sipping a little sake
with my old friend, Tu Fu.

Our capital is overrun and occupied
by human vermin
spreading misery and ecocide.

I will not get drunk before
I go to bed. There is little
to celebrate, little to be said.

The ancient maestro bows his head
knowingly. Empire is made
of sand, not stone,

and the waters come deep and wide.
Gate, gate, paragate.
Nowhere to run, nowhere to hide.

Salutations to another year
turned slowly into dust, another year
to enlighten and bedevil us.

Samuel Hazo
To a Commencement of Scoundrels

My boys, we lied to you.
The world by definition stinks
of Cain, no matter what
your teachers told you. Heroes
and the fools of God may rise
like accidental green
on gray saharas, but the sand
stays smotheringly near.

Deny me if you can. Already
you are turning into personnel,
manpower, figures on a list
of earners, voters, prayers,
soldiers, payers, sums
of population tamed with forms:
last name, middle name, first name—
telephone—date of birth—

home address—age—hobbies—
experience. Tell them the truth.
Your name is Legion. You
are aged a million. Tell
them that. Say you breathe
between appointments: first day,
last day. The rest is no
one's business. Boys, the time

is prime for prophecy.
Books break down their bookends.
Paintings burst their frames.
The world is more than reason's
peanut. Homer sang it real,
Goya painted it, and Shakespeare
staged it for the pelting rinds
of every groundling of the Globe.

Wake up! Tonight the lions
hunt in Kenya. They
can eat a man. Rockets
are spearing through the sky.
They can blast a man to nothing.
Rumors prowl like rebellions.
They can knife a man. No one
survives for long, my boys.

Flesh is always in season:
lusted after, gunned, grenaded,
tabulated through machines,
incinerated, beaten to applause,
anesthetized, autopsied, mourned.
The blood of Troy beats on
in Goya's paintings and the truce
of Lear. Reason yourselves

to that, my buckaroos,
before you rage for God,
country, and siss-boom-bah!
You won't, of course. Your schooling
left you trained to serve
like cocksure Paul before
God's lightning smashed
him from his saddle. So—
I wish you what I wish
myself: hard questions
and the nights to answer them,
the grace of disappointment
and the right to seem the fool
for justice. That's enough.
Cowards might ask for more.
Heroes have died for less.

Marcelo Hernandez Castillo
Field Guide Ending in a Deportation

I confess to you my inadequacies. I want to tell you things I do not know about myself. I've made promises to people whom I will never see again. I've cried in an airport bathroom stall in El Paso, Texas, when immigration denied my father's application. It felt like a mathematical equation—everything on one side needed to equal everything on the other. It almost made sense to be that sad. I am not compelled to complicate this metaphor. I'm selling this for two dollars. Years ago, on my birthday, I came out to my friends. I thought about the possibility of painting their portraits. What a stupid idea. I've started to cover up certain words with Barbie stickers in my journal. It occurs to me, sitting in my car at a Dollar General parking lot, in search of cheap balloons for a party which I do not care about, that I am allowed my own joy. I pick the brightest balloons, pay, drive home, and dress for the party. I mouth the words *happy birthday to you* in a dark room lit by everyone's phone cameras. Afterward, I enter all of my emails from five years into a cloud engine and the most used word is *ok*. I confess that I have had a good life. I spend many nights obsessing over the placement of my furniture. I give you my boredom. I give you my obligation. I give you the night I danced and danced and danced at a child's birthday party, drunk and by myself. I've been someone else's shame. It's true, at its core, amá was deported because she was hit by a car. For years to come, this will be the ending of a sad joke she likes to tell. I laugh each time she tells the joke to strangers. Something about how there is more metal than bone in her arm. Something about a magnet. She says, *I thought I had died and death meant repeating a name forever.* She says, *El jardín encierra la boca de mis pasos.* But this is a bad translation. It's more like, *I felt like a star, I felt like somebody famous.*

Juan Felipe Herrera
We Are Remarkably Loud Not Masked

young Jesse Washington—
            even though you   on the wooden stick
cross of fire bitten charred cut & burned   5 minute jury
April 15, 1916, Waco, Texas, shackled & dragged—lynched
            you live on

                Trayvon Martin face down
red juice on the lawn clutching candy rushing home
the hoodie the hoodie the prowler shooter said
upside down shredded night

                because of you you
we march touch hands lean back leap forth
against the melancholy face of tanks & militia   we move
                walk become
we become   somehow
Eric Garner we scribble your name sip your breath   now
        our breath cannot be choked off our
skin cannot be flamed   totality
                cannot be cut off
each wrist
each bone
cannot be chained to the abyss
        gnashing levers & polished
            killer sheets of steel

we are remarkably loud not masked
        rough river colors that cannot be threaded back
hear us
Freddie Gray here   with us

            Jesse Washington Trayvon Martin
Michael Brown the Black Body holy
        Eric Garner all breath Holy

we weep & sing
as we write

     as we mobilize & march
         under the jubilant solar face

Jane Hirshfield
On the Fifth Day

January 24, 2017

On the fifth day
the scientists who studied the rivers
were forbidden to speak
or to study the rivers.

The scientists who studied the air
were told not to speak of the air,
and the ones who worked for the farmers
were silenced,
and the ones who worked for the bees.

Someone, from deep in the Badlands,
began posting facts.

The facts were told not to speak
and were taken away.
The facts, surprised to be taken, were silent.

Now it was only the rivers
that spoke of the rivers,
and only the wind that spoke of its bees,

while the unpausing factual buds of the fruit trees
continued to move toward their fruit.

The silence spoke loudly of silence,
and the rivers kept speaking
of rivers, of boulders and air.

Bound to gravity, earless and tongueless,
the untested rivers kept speaking.

Bus drivers, shelf stockers,
code writers, machinists, accountants,
lab techs, cellists kept speaking.

They spoke, the fifth day,
of silence.

Jane Hirshfield
Let Them Not Say

Let them not say: we did not see it.
We saw.

Let them not say: we did not hear it.
We heard.

Let them not say: they did not taste it.
We ate, we trembled.

Let them not say: it was not spoken, not written.
We spoke,
we witnessed with voices and hands.

Let them not say: they did nothing.
We did not-enough.

Let them say, as they must say something:

A kerosene beauty.
It burned.

Let them say we warmed ourselves by it,
read by its light, praised,
and it burned.

Everett Hoagland
Georgia on His Mind

At the bar
the black man
picks up his glass

the way he picked cotton.
Gin oils Eli Whitney's machine.

His tongue is cotton;
his mind a cotton gin;
his life, a mill wheel on
the river, oils the machine.

His soul is a boll weevil.

Everett Hoagland
At the Access

In loving memory of my parents,
Everett and Estelle Hoagland

The view is always renewed. Today
as I descended the weathered steps of the lake
access, I paused to look at shadowed Champlain
—and remembered
"Points of Interest" in the staid, old Essex Inn's
new brochure: the bay is four hundred feet deep
far out, off nearby Town Park Beach. At the bottom
I wondered

who walked in, fell in, jumped in, went
under to lake bed long ago. Who drowned
among the Native Peoples, early French,
the sport fishermen, canoeing tourists,
heedless, headstrong children? Whose

were the accidental deaths, recurrent,
despairing suicides? Something unseen
splashed. The whispering water's low waves, ripples,
lapped the pebbled shore, distorting my reflection
as I stood there barefoot, ankle deep, on the edge

I sank
into deep, dark, cold silence; a sullen
city frame of reference made the mirroring
water more than forty stories deep. . . .

. . . A black loon surfaced,
a small shiny fish sideways
in its beak; shook its feathers dry;
shook and headfirst swallowed its stilled, quick-
silver prey.

The wind picked up; the softwoods' new leaves showed
their silvered undersides. The pines swished hushes

overhead. A brown duck's alarming squawk
and sudden flight across my bay

of years to boyhood, across the centuries'
settlements, aboriginal millennia, the glacial lake's ice
ages and thaws brought me to see me
and the water for what we were, what we are, what we will,
can be, again, all that. I gazed at, contemplated
Champlain's tiered mountain backdrop.

Squatted, searched,
picked up a thin, flat stone; watched it skip
the water over and over and over again after
my windup and curled-finger pitch, skills—
like bike balance, fishing, swimming
—learned for life.

I stared across the great lake and heard the silent
visual fugue of Vermont's undulant Green
Mountains; pushed off
taking tackle box and other gear; rowed
my little childhood boat
toward them across the suddenly still waters
and hummed a hymn.

Lawrence Joseph
Here in a State of Tectonic Tension

Its geography similar to Istanbul's—
read for Lake Huron, the Black Sea,
for the St. Clair River, the Bosporus,
for Lake St. Clair, the Sea of Marmara,
for the Detroit River, the Dardanelles,
and for Lake Erie, the Mediterranean—
a natural place for Ford and Olds to open factories,
strategically near the Pittsburgh steel mills, Akron
rubber plants, Mesabi iron ore range.
Here, in ultimate concentration, is industrial
America—Chrysler, Continental, Budd, Hudson,
in an area not much larger than two square miles,
ninety to a hundred thousand employed on two
or three shifts—the capital of a new planet, the one
on wheels. Whacked-out, stamped-out connecting rods,
the steady blown-out flare of furnaces, hammer die
brought down on anvil die, oil-holes drilled and oil-
grooves cut—Fordism was Gramsci's word to describe
mass assembly based on systems of specialized
machines operating within organizational domains
of vertically integrated conglomerates fed by small
and medium-sized units coordinated by methods
of marketing exchange—an epical, systemic violence.
Anonymous's eyes pop as he laughs and says
"dragged the old coon from his car, kicked him till
he shit himself, and then we set the auto on fire—God
Jesus was it a show!" How many summers after that
the Motor City burned to the ground? Soon several new
regimes of redistributed wealth would alter the way
capitalism proceeded, a squad of police breaks down
the union hall door, swinging crowbars and tossing canisters
of Mace—around the time the long depression started.
There are stalks of weeds in sunlit snow, an abandoned
house surrounded by acres of snow. The decay apparently
has frightened the smart money away. Metaphorically
underwater—more is owed on properties in Detroit than
they're worth. His hands and feet were bound, found

beaten in a field near Post and Fort, he's in intensive
care at Receiving Hospital, says Sergeant Ollie L. Atkins,
investigators yet to ask him who he is or what happened.
Notice that on the high school baseball diamond is a herd
of goats—attended by whom? Notice, a few doors down,
the stucco-plastered house painted baby blue, walking in front
in a red stocking cap, green specks on his shoes—what
do you think he is thinking? Drive Woodward to Seven Mile,
west on Seven Mile to Hamilton, Hamilton south to the Lodge
Freeway, then the Lodge downtown, and measure the chaos,
drive Mack Avenue east to Seminole, south on Seminole
to Charlevoix, then west on Charlevoix to Van Dyke, south
on Van Dyke to East Jefferson, and remember what isn't.
Ionic pillars carved with grapes and vine leaves no longer
there, deserted houses of gigantic bulk, in which it seems
incredible anyone could ever have lived, no longer there,
Dodge Main's nocturnal gold vapors no longer there,
the constellated bright lights reflected on the Rouge River's
surface no longer there. Narco-capital techno-compressed,
gone viral, spread into a state of tectonic tension and freaky
abstractions—it'll scare the fuck out of you, is what it'll do,
anthropomorphically scaled down by the ferocity of its own
obsolescence. Which of an infinity of reasons explain it?
Which of an infinity of conflagrations implode its destruction?

Lawrence Joseph
Visions of Labor

I will have writings written all over it
   in human words: wrote Blake. A running
form, Pound's Blake: shouting, whirling
   his arms, his eyes rolling, whirling like flaming
cartwheels. Put it this way, in this language:
   a blow in the small of the back from a rifle butt,
the crack of a blackjack on a skull, face
   beaten to a pulp, punched in the nose
with a fist, glasses flying off, "fuckin' Wobbly
   wop, hit him again for me," rifle barrel slammed
against the knees, so much blood in the eyes,
   rain, and the night, and the shooting pain
all up and down the spine, can't see. Put it
   this way: in the sense of smell is an acrid
odor of scorched metal, in the sense of sound,
   the roaring of blowtorches. Put it in this
language: labor's value is abstract value,
   abstracted into space in which a milling machine
cutter cuts through the hand, the end of her thumb
   nearly sliced off, metal shavings driven in, rapidly
infected. Put it at this point, the point at which
   capital is most inhumane, unsentimental,
out of control: the quantity of human labor in
   the digital manufacture of a product is progressing
toward the economic value of zero, the maintenance
   and monitoring of new cybernetic processes
occupied by fungible, commodified, labor
   in a form of indentured servitude. Static model,
dynamic model, alternate contract environments,
   enterprise size and labor market functions,
equilibrium characterization, elasticity of response
   to productivity shocks: the question in this Third
Industrial Revolution is who owns and controls
   the data. That's what we're looking at, labor cheap,
replaceable, self-replicating, marginal, contracted out
   into smaller and smaller units. Them? Hordes
of them, of depleted economic, social value,

who don't count, in any situation, in anyone's eyes,
and won't count, ever, no matter what, the truth that,
    sooner than later, one way or another, they will simply
die off. In Hanover Square, a freezing dawn,
    inside bronze doors the watchman sips bourbon
and black coffee from a paper cup, sees a drunk or drugged
    hedge fund boy step over a passed-out body. Logic
of exploitation. Logic of submission; alienation.
    Eyes fixed on mediated screens, in semiotic
labor flow: how many generations between
    the age of slavery of these States and ours?
Makers we, of perfectly contemplated machines.

Yusef Komunyakaa
A Prayer for Workers

Bless the woman, man, & child
    who honor Earth by opening shine
inside the soil—the splayed hour
    between dampness & dust—to plant
seedlings in double furrows, & then pray
    for cooling rain. Bless the fields,
the catch, the hunt, & the wild fruit,
    & let no one go hungry tonight
or tomorrow. Let the wind & birds
    seed a future ferried into villages
& towns the other side of mountains
    along nameless rivers. Bless those
born with hands made to grapple
    hewn timbers & stone raised from earth
& shaped in circles, who know the geometry
    of corners, & please level the foundation
& pitch a roof so good work isn't diminished
    by rain. Bless the farmer with clouds
in his head, who lugs baskets of dung
    so termites can carve their hives
that hold water long after a downpour
    has gone across the desert & seeds
sprout into a contiguous greening.
    Bless the iridescent beetle working
to haul the heavens down, to journey
    from red moon dust to excrement.
The wage slave two steps from Dickens's
    tenements among a den of thieves,
blind soothsayers who know shambles
    where migrants feathered the nests
of straw bosses as the stonecutters
    perfect profiles of robber barons
in granite & marble in town squares
    along highways paved for Hollywood.
Bless souls laboring in sweatshops,
    & each calabash dipper of water,
the major & minor litanies & ganglia

dangling from promises at the mouth
of the cave, the catcher of vipers at dawn
in the canebrake & flowering fields,
not for love of money but for bread
& clabber on a thick gray slab table,
for the simple blessings in a hamlet
of the storytellers drunk on grog.
Bless the cobbler, molding leather
on his oaken lasts, kneading softness
& give into a red shoe & a work boot,
never giving more to one than the other,
& also the weaver with closed eyes
whose fingers play the ties & loops
as if nothing else matters, daybreak
to sunset, as gritty stories of a people
grow into an epic stitched down
through the ages, the outsider artists
going from twine & hue, cut & tag,
an ironmonger's credo of steam rising
from buckets & metal dust, & the clang
of a hammer against an anvil,
& the ragtag ones, a whole motley crew
at the end of the line, singing ballads
& keeping time on a battered tin drum.

Yusef Komunyakaa
The Mushroom Gatherers

The hard work of love sealed
in language has stolen me far
from home, from the fields,
& I see morning mist rising
where they borrow ghosts
to get even with each other,
harvesting vegetable fruit
close as we can get to dirt.
I glimpse shadows smudged
in trees lining the highway
where night & day commingle,
or as a season moves slow this hour,
saying, Bad things happened here.
At first, the figures seem to be
staring into earth, like migrants
who work Florida & California,
unearthing what we live to eat.

We know the men from women
by the colors they wear, sweat
ringing their lives in gray shade,
& our bus makes the mushroom
gatherers with pails & canvas bags
blur among the trees as if shutters
are opening & closing, as the mind
runs to keep up. But the road forks
here in eastern Europe, & I hardly
can see faces in the door of leaves.
The women know where to stand
in the clearing, how each trucker
slows down to make the curve,
& cannot miss yellow or purple.
He honks his loud bluesy horn,
idling at the bottom of the hill
on a thin shoulder of blacktop.

Dorianne Laux
If It Weren't for Bad Ideas, I'd Have No Ideas at All

A bad idea is like a road we go down
at dusk, passing each lit gas station
thinking it won't be the last, as if home
could be anywhere behind us, any grief
we don't need, like the chipped knife
in the glove box, the month of December
with its cold stars, its end-of-the-world trees.

We forget to pack a jacket, down or tweed:
no dinner parties, no search parties, just you
and your burning, your Big Because,
a boom beneath that could be a bald tire
giving up, the resonant sound in your brain
saying, *Keep going, ride on the rims.*

Adrian C. Louis
Skinology

Yellow roses, wild roses,
their decades of growth,
a fierce fence between
the drunkenness
of my neighbors
& me.

***

I have known
some badass Skins.
Clichéd bad-to-the-bone
Indians who were maybe
not bad but just broke,
& broken for sure.

***

Late winter, late night,
a gentle rapping, a tapping
on my chamber door . . .
some guy selling a block
of commodity cheese
for five bucks.

***

You climbed a tree,
sat there for hours
until some kind voice
called you back home.
You unfolded your wings,
took to the air & smashed
into earth. They hauled
you to ER, then Detox
where they laughed
at your broken wings.

Once, I thought
I saw eagles soar,
loop *&* do the crow hop
in the blue air while
the sun beat the earth
like a drum, but I was
disheveled *&* drinking
those years.

***

Indians *&* the internet.
Somewhere, sometime.
Whenever a Messiah
Chief is born, jealous
relatives will drag him
down like the old days
only instantly now.

***

In a brutal land
within a brutal land
with corrupt leaders
& children killing themselves
we know who is to blame.
But we are on a train,
a runaway train *&* we
don't know what to do.

***

The good earth,
the sun blazing down,
us in our chones, butts
stuck in inner tubes,
floating down a mossy
green river, speechless,
stunned silent with joy

& sobriety & youth,
oh youth.

***

She smiled at me
& got off her horse.
She smelled of leather
& sweat & her kiss has
lasted me fifty years.

***

Bad Indians do
not go to hell.
They are marched
to the molten core
of the sun & then
beamed back to
their families,
purified, whole
& Holy as hell.

Adrian C. Louis
Invisible Places of Refuge

Deep inside myself,
I am running out
of places to hide.
I am an old man,
a dirty old man &
the world we knew
is fading fast away.
I cannot say how I
became covered with
the cobwebs common
to poor & broken folk.
Darling, I cannot say
if I'm spider or fly.

***

My love, I pray that you
can not see me now, but
of course you can see me
& yes, I am a walking scar,
one of life's miracles, but
you're just a ghost, still,
the only ghost that I
dream hard about.
I will never hide from
the hauntings you offer.

***

Soon I will need no
invisible places of refuge.
While other spirits float
through a dire dampness
of tears & wet kisses, I
will flitter about, brittle &
arid as a pack of Top Ramen.

***

How I love my Top Ramen.
Top Ramen is my hemlock.
It shrinks my body & soul.
My body has grown thin
& my shadow so skeletal
that it often hides from me
& the palaces of memory,
from all that I've known.
Dear Gods of my known
& unknown universes.
I thank you for the sweet,
sweet & holy miracle
of noodles made from
the baked & pulverized
bones of poor folk.

Adrian C. Louis
The Motherland

Election Night, 2016

Pallid folks, both guided
& misguided bump uglies
& exchange vows against
a backdrop of dirges sung
by millions of dark men
seething behind steel bars.
Pallid folks are bored with
the old songs of pain & are
thankful that the cold heart
of democracy, sliced thinly,
has fed them for centuries.
Sieg Heil, Mama-jammers.
Sieg Heil, Flim-flammers.

Ricardo Alberto Maldonado
I Give You My Heart / Os doy mi corazón

I find myself on my feet with fifteen leaves.
Everything carries its own light on the walls.

I woke up being hit. The afternoon,
suffocating as the death of cows. My heart
was opened between cemeteries of moon.

The parasites. The drizzle. The mud crowning
the undergrowth with immense sadness.

I knew death when I dressed
in my uniform.

I found the index of solitude: my country in its legal
jargon, its piety, its fiction—

Yes. It loves me, really.

I give my blood as the blood of all fish.

*

Me encuentro de pie con quince hojas.
Brilla todo en los muros.

Desperté al ser golpeado. La tarde,
asfixiante como la muerte de vacas. Mi corazón
lo abrían entre cementerios de luna.

Los parásitos. La llovizna. El lodo coronando
la maleza con mustios grandes.

Supe de la muerte al vestir
de uniforme.

Encontré el índice de soledad: mi país en su jerga
legal, su piedad, su ficción—

Sí. Me quiere, de verdad.

Doy mi sangre como la sangre de todos los peces.

Paul Mariani
The Girl Who Learned to Sing in Crow

Plash of water from the kitchen sink, a spotless
blue sky eastering through the open window
above the gleaming faucet, and a fistful of buttercups
plucked by their tender stems from along

the border of our rusting fence, placed just so
along the white formica sill as if framed.
An image of my sister's still life—*nature
morte*—as once more the mind's eye

catches her washing a heap of dishes
like the little mother she used to think she was,
as she sang softly to herself, like some blind
canary that sings because it must. Ah,

how she sang with all the bright abandon
of her tender years, long and softly, though her brothers,
not knowing what to make of such graceful notes,
mocked and mimicked her with counter song, *caw! caw!*

No need now to rehearse the pressures there
to stun and stunt a voice. The truth is that
even now I cannot bring myself to say it all.
Call it the pockmarked havoc of our growing up.

Call it whatever name you bloody please.
It's all behind us, we tell ourselves. And who wants
to take the blame for the silence which says so well
how we treat our women? How we mock them for

the very courage we ourselves gasp after in our locked
and airless rooms. Or sacrifice their hopes to men
stronger than ourselves, slapping back and rump
in winking fellowship, so that, as one day yields

to yet another, we still catch glimpses of a scrawny
girl learning how to split her tongue and caw.
Hell, we know it happens all the time. We know
just as they do it's the songbirds make good eating.

Paul Mariani
Ghost

After so much time you'd think
you'd have it netted
in the mesh of language. But again
it reconfigures, slick as Proteus.

You're in the kitchen talking
with your ex-Navy brother, his two kids
snaking over his tattooed arms, as he goes on
& on about being out of work again.

For an hour now you've listened,
his face growing dimmer in the lamplight
as you keep glancing at your watch
until it's there again: the ghost rising

as it did that first time when you,
the oldest, left home to marry.
You're in the boat again, alone, and staring
at the six of them, your sisters

& your brothers, their faces bobbing
in the water, as their fingers grapple
for the gunwales. The ship is going down,
your mother with it. One oar's locked

and feathered, and one oar's lost,
there's a slop of gurry pooling
in the bottom, and your tiny boat
keeps drifting further from them.

Between each bitter wave you can count
their upturned faces—white roses
scattered on a mash of sea, eyes fixed
to see what you will do. And you?

You their old protector, you their guardian
and go-between? *Each man for himself,*
you remember thinking, their faces
growing dimmer with each oar stroke.

Paul Mariani
Mexico

It will be the last time the U.S. Cavalry
will use horses in combat. Spads, Fokkers,
machine guns, tanks: all will see to that.
My grandfather is nineteen and hails from
Paterson, the filthy Passaic the river
he knows best. Now it's the Rio Grande
that greets him and his army-issue horse
whose name is Red. That much I know.
Harry. Harry Szymborski or Sembeski
or Sembooki, or however the census takers
spelled his name, what the hell difference
did it make? His parents worked the mills
along the Falls as weavers and machinists,
grinding work, and why he joined the army.
Five eight, brown eyes, brown hair, bantam-
weight, so the records say. In the photo
I have of him he's excised his face
so the eye can focus on his horse.

It's April, 1916, and he's part of the Expedition
going after Villa. He's saddled up and his carbine
glints, and soon he will be heading south
from Texas into Mexico after a shadow
the army will never capture. Through endless arid
days and deserts, past blossoming cacti
and blue fevered skies and serpentine arroyos,
past the chalk-dry bones of men and cattle
flowing ghostlike backward by him,
he floats as in a dream, the language strange
and those who live there stranger, one
more U.S. soldier awakening to another
twilight nightmare: Okinawa, the Chosin
Reservoir, Khe Sanh, and Kuwait's smoldering
oil fields, then Kabul, until at last one arrives
in the Land of JubJub, one more Polish kid
following orders, one more benighted knight

sent out to make the world safe, at least for oil,
trudging back to Texas, then on to France,
where mustard gas will get him, having done
his part to end the war to end all wars until
the next one calls, and then the next, and
the twilit borders bleed together, as he goes on
doing what he must, until at last the very road
he rides upon with Red his horse will have
long since turned to dust along with him.

Demetria Martínez
Inauguration Day, 2017

A Mexican nun
told me: refry beans
with a touch of milk if
you don't have lard.
Remember that, friends,
write it down, write down
all such tips from those
who lived in times like
these, who knew to add
more onion for flavor, still
more onion to stretch a meal.
We have many mouths to feed.
Many signs to paint, miles
to march. Coffee to
brew for meetings that
melt into the night. Sit down.
We can always make room.
Beans, tortillas, calabacitas,
chile verde. You're home now.
Hold hands, our blessing
is simple: pass the pepper,
pass the salt.

Paul Martínez Pompa
MyKillAdoreHer

That Lucia broke the machine twice in one week was evidence enough. He also offered this—she's no longer automatic, her stitches are crooked and once another seamstress found Lucia's "lost" sewing patterns in the trash. The security guard half listened as Lucia gathered her things. Then the manager turned directly to her—what is it with you? We give you work, put money in your pocket. She put on her best face as they escorted her past rows of itchy throats, bowed heads, the refrain of needle through fabric.

*

Every day Elena counts pig. A pageant of molded plastic rolling down the conveyor belt. The task: grab Miss Piggy, pull gown over snout, fasten two tiny buttons, grab another. With each doll Elena's hands grow stiffer. Her feet grow heavy as the concrete below. Dolls spit at her, or maybe this is imagined, but the ache in her legs might be real. The supervisor brushes against her back when he patrols the floor. After standing for hours, the room begins to blur. Her mouth opens like an empty wallet. The naked dolls march on.

*

What will settle in, what will rise from the lungs of girls who still burn weeks after detox treatment at a local clinic. Tales of headaches, blurred vision, diarrhea. How they suck air thick with sulfuric acid. Acetone working past unfiltered exhaust systems and through their livers. Most return to work despite doctors' orders. Back inside, the tin roof and their steady sweat remind them they're still alive. Together one breathing, burning machine.

*

Like Celia's pockets, there's nothing but lint here. Lint & dead machines. The sound of layoffs & profit margins. Yesterday this department droned an unsynchronized rhythm of coughing girls tethered to well-lubed motors. Row after row of pre-asthmatic lungs. Black hair buried under perpetual white. The decision was made across the border, he tells them. Nothing I can do about it. Sometimes Celia would imagine the whole place caught inside a tiny globe. Something she could pick up. Shake. Destroy.

A perpetual conveyor, he patrols her mouth. The sound of unfiltered white. Breathing margins. The task: grab Elena's hands. Pull. Fasten. He also offered crooked patterns. Put money in her hair. That Lucia broke. Was evidence enough? Molded vision as a refrain. An empty wallet will rise. Speak. How they exhaust systems. Despite the blurred other, the ache might be real. Something she could pick up. Across the border, nothing I can imagine.

Paul Martínez Pompa
Framework

The elder man's eyes tell a story
his mouth is reluctant to share,

but the trees that line his block go talking,
up and down the entire city:

not *if* they will see death
but when. Not *if* leaves will fall,

but how. It is true—
last night, on this block,

a young man caught a bullet
behind his eye. He will live

but carry lead until some future light
when his soul is pulled skyward

into the next song of life and death.
Yes, last night, bullets let loose

toward a stoop of young men, neighbors
froze behind windows, police

hung yellow tape and tripods held up
cameras thirsty for death.

Yes, it happened here, last night.
But today, there is a tree that needs to be climbed.

There is a front lawn that needs to be cut.
There are dogs that need to be walked up and down

the sidewalk and *that* is what's breathing.
Here. Now.

Today it's back to work & play.
Someplace else, there is a frame, a longing

for trends that turn the people against the people.
We've been trained for a narrative

of blood, which isn't untrue but isn't
complete. This is a block too alive for framework.

It is lined with brick homes that stand
prouder than lead, and children

who need no lessons in how to be
children, and elders who walk a line

between saying and not saying
until their dreams sing into fruition. This

is a gathering
of the living and the working

and the playing and the dying.
They are what move this city, every day,

beyond the framework that bends truth,
beneath the trees that don't.

Julio Marzán
Don't Let Me Die in Disneyland

Don't let me die in Disneyland,
where camera-posed
under Donald Duck's hug
and canopy beak
children don't see
the cloud pirate ship
of black cotton candy,
where sniffing me Pluto
picks up no scent,
and Goofy's too smart
to trip on a speed bump
he knows is just me.

Don't let me die in Disneyland,
where buckskin Crockett
aims his supremacy
at infantry-uniformed
Mexican clowns,
where home from the mine
Snow White's seven dwarfs
all claim to be Dopey
and dance around Hi Ho!
as off to death I go.

Don't let me die in Disneyland,
where Jiminy Cricket
chirps not at all
and Pinocchio's nose
stays thimble small
despite his big lie
I never was there,
Lost Boy who lost
every happy thought
and fell from his flight
to Never Never Land
and had to grow up.

Don't let me die in Disneyland,
where in gunpowder night
fireworks awe
blooms to illumine
Cinderella Castle
but not the crossbones
of a black hull,
its treasure my corpse,
unseen above Main Street
as in Grand Master tux,
a trumpet for scepter,
Mickey Mouse leads
the American Parade.

Marty McConnell
White Girl Interrogates Her Own Heart Again

Shut the door. Outside, the newspapers fly themselves
against the stone and glass until the light stops. Come,
my little contradictory multichambered thudder.
Take the chair closest to the radiator. We love
our small comforts. Our lavender tea and quiet

boulevard. No one is blaming you
for these. Soldiers in all wars lean into
their vices, and I know that you hate war. But war
is here. Is you. Is our brilliant city, on fire even

as we speak. Is a flag we take to the back porch
to wring out softly, before family arrives.
So as not to discuss the blood. So as not
to discomfort those who made us. But heart, oh

heart. Discomfort is the weapon we bring to this
needful table. Without you, we are all statistic
or fist. Without you, more and more fire. Look
how the wind disturbs the curtains through
the closed window. Look how it finds a way in.

Marty McConnell
The Sacrament of Penance

I come to claim the white boy who yesterday slaughtered nine Black worshippers at prayer. Because to deny him is to deny the ways he and I are the same, deny the hideous lineage that dogs us and feeds us. Gavel and spit. Rope and bumper and chain. I claim him but will not say his name. It slips down my throat like half-gone milk, slick and hard.

I come to claim the white father who gave his white boy a gun for turning 21. I claim him as my own dripping shadow, as my own burning sanctuary. I claim him with his wife, I put their names in a bucket and fill it with tar. I fill it with bleach. I fill it with salt and light it on fire. I put my name in there too, but always it comes back to me. Covered in asphalt. Covered in newsprint. Covered in grief.

I come to claim my gods who are your God who are all the winds that rise in arcing rage at what is taken, at what is taken, at what is never returned. I say wind but mean gale. I say gale but mean storm. I say storm but mean bloodsquall, I mean what is brewing will boil. It will bitter. It will burn, and burn, and these white tears kerosene on the blaze.

Marty McConnell
The Sacrament of Hope after Despair

How many men must we survive? The forty-something at the screen door when I was 15. Roses on the porch whenever Dad was out of town. The one who tried to rape me. The other one who tried to rape me. The one who lied and dissolved and lied and dissolved and lied until I left, then followed me home to lie again. The one who made me and broke my mother's heart. The ones with the perfect syllables concealing machetes. Getting hard pursuing ruin. The ones with the gun racks and sweet guitars.The ones rolling promotions in their suit pant pockets like loose change. The ones who lisp Audre Lorde quotes over top shelf bourbon as if the beds they rose from to come here aren't full of women who used to have hands. Not all men, but enough. Enough.

> Oh my nephews. Oh my godson.
> You do not have to be women
> to be kind. Look at your fathers, wounded
> by their own fathering, how they make
> tea and hold you. Destroying
> nothing. Killing no one.

Leslie McGrath
Rage Bracelet

Women create the beast to know
the depth of their desire

every prison wants a warden
every tablecloth a stain

A matched set of bruises
at the collarbone   round the wrist

every guru wants a devotee
every amulet a chain

Women forgive the beast and learn
the depth of their despair

every landscape wants a shadow
every abattoir a drain

Leslie McGrath
When Dividing the Unbelievable by the Undeniable

Coarse as sand   the thief in a slick red tie
sticks his slick red tongue   into your ear

You can still hear   but you don't believe
what you're hearing   Who took sandpaper

to the truth   and roughed up   its smooth surface?
Capricious molecules   wobble round private suns

in private galaxies   where private parties
disclose nothing   but unbelievable cruelty

Yet what is unbelievable is still divisible
neutrinos   news organizations   nations

Look at cruelty   don't deny it   you want to
look at it   garish & underwhelming   stained golden

a fool's gold   a gold divisible   as a fraction
you cannot solve   but you can refuse

to let it move you   Be not afraid   Be not afraid
Lean against the coarsening with all your might.

Richard Michelson
Gossip Is Forbidden

the rabbi said, peering over his bifocals. If you steal goods
or money you can repent and repay, but not so the evil tongue.
Permission to shoplift is what we, at fifteen, heard, high-fiving
outside the synagogue door. Catch us if you can—we'll atone
in fifty years if any one of us is left alive. Today at sixty-five
I see three teens pocketing chocolates from the neighborhood

market, stuffing their stylish kangaroo-pouch Patagonia hoodies
with ninety-two percent dark Ghirardelli plus boxes of Good
& Plenty pink candy. I start to speak, then, biting my tongue,
wind it back into the clammy dankness of its mucosa-lined cave.
One boy turns, sees me seeing and freezes until the ringtone
of his iPhone breaks the spell. The tableau instantly comes alive,

each of us playing our part. And you, dear reader, who are still alive,
need to know that in The Year of Our Lord, 2017, white-hooded
hoodlums marched through Charlottesville, Virginia, intoning
"Jew will not replace us" and our President said there were good
and bad apples, bigots, and "very fine people" on both sides. Tongue-
tied, I cannot believe what my ears have heard, so I replay those five

words again in my mind: "Jew will not replace us." When I was five,
my grandfather reprimanded my new first-grade schoolmates with five
words of his own: "Words hurt worse than stones." His mother-tongue
was Yiddish, and I was shamed by his accented appeal to the brotherhood
of White America. I'd already heard *kike* and *Christ-killer* and the Good
Friday prayer for the "perfidious Jews." For years I spoke a monotone

to distance myself from those excitable Semites whose dark skin tones
proved—until it didn't—then did again—that they would never be saved.
A curse could kill, my grandmother knew, so she stayed silent at Good-
will working us into the mainstream, her prayers parting seas, saving
us with each penny saved. Thank God she didn't live to see herself hood-
winked. Behind the bars of her teeth, guarded by lips, her tongue,

locked up like a murderer serving a life sentence, stills my own tongue
as these three boys saunter down the aisle. Defying the overtones
of racism—one boy Latino, two black—the Pakistani earning his livelihood
behind the counter pulls out a gun. And here again we freeze, all five
posed like a Ghirlandaio fresco, when, straight from the mouth of the cave,
Jesus, resurrected, walks through the open door. I bring you The Good

News, he babbles, speaking in tongues. He picks up and pockets a Good
Land apple. O, my undocumented rabbi, I intone, what parable can save
us? *Beresh't* was falsehood and truth, he says. Speak, my children, and live.

Richard Michelson
Fake News

"My throte is kut unto my nekke boon"

When the president's spokesperson coined the term *alternative facts*
to replace *blatant lies,* my Facebook feed went crazy. I'm writing a poem
titled "Fake News" one "friend" said, but another cautioned: *Too topical;*
It will be fish-wrap in days and no one will know what you're talking about.
But I'm still stuck on Saint William of Norwich, the apprentice tanner
found dead in the twelfth century on the corner of Cruelty and Credulity
while the monk, Thomas of Monmouth, concocted a blood libel, blaming
the ritual murder—*to flavor their matzo*—on the Jews; martyred, the boy
would end up on this panel of painted oak in London's Victoria and Albert,
where I'm sitting on a bench checking my brand-new Verizon smartphone
for the latest evidence in support of my political views. I'm reading clickbait
instead of *The Canterbury Tales,* so not till tonight, will I recall that Chaucer,
two hundred years later, would spread the same vile libel through the lips
of his Prioress; her poetry, a far more persuasive and timeless fiction.

E. Ethelbert Miller
Still Life in Black

Outside the museums black
homeless men sleep on benches

Black plastic bags their only
possessions

E. Ethelbert Miller
What Do They Do?

What do torturers do when they return home?
Do they make love to their wives and play with their kids?
What hobbies do they have?
Do they wash the car and take out the trash?
Do they change their underwear?
What do torturers see when they look in the refrigerator?
When shopping do they go to the front of the line?
Do they get discounts on meat?
Do torturers remember their anniversaries?
Do they place candles on birthday cakes and blow them out?
When torturers go to church who do they pray to?
When they get caught in traffic jams do they curse the cars in front of them?
Do they worry when they get dirt and blood under their fingernails?
What type of deodorant do they use?
When torturers leave a room do they turn out the lights?
Are they superstitious?
Do they avoid stepping on sidewalk cracks?
Do they read their horoscopes before going to work?
How many torturers have two jobs?
When lost do they ask strangers for directions?
Are they left-handed or right-handed?
Do torturers sit in outdoor cafes and talk about torture?
Do they suffer memory loss?
Do they call in sick and say they can't report for work?
How safe is a torturer's workplace?
When they fall to sleep do they snore?
Do torturers keep everyone awake at night?

E. Ethelbert Miller
Bunting and the Art of Nonviolence

All your life you played small ball.
In elementary school you held the door
open for your teacher. This taught you
the art of bunting and kind manners.
You sacrificed being first so someone
could reach second. Once returning
to the dugout Gandhi slapped your butt
and said "good job."
He also said "the bat is not a club."

Kamilah Aisha Moon
Fannie Lou Hamer

"I'm sick and tired of being sick and tired!"

She sat across the desk from me, squirming.
It was stifling. My suite runs hot
but most days it is bearable.

This student has turned in nothing,
rarely comes to class. When she does,
her eyes bore into me with a disdain
born long before either of us.

She doesn't trust anything I say.
She can't respect my station,
the words coming out of these lips,
this face. My breathing
is an affront. *It's me*, she says.

I never was this student's professor—
her immediate reaction
seeing me at the SMART board.
But I have a calling to complete
& she has to finish college,
return to a town where
she doesn't have to look at,
listen to or respect anyone
like me—forever tall, large
& brown in her dagger eyes,
though it's clear she looks down
on me. She can return—
if not to her hometown, another
enclave, so many others, where
she can brush a dog's golden coat,
be vegan & call herself
a good person.

Are you having difficulty with your other classes?

No.

Go, I say, tenderly.
Loaded as a cop's gun,
she blurts point-blank
that she's *afraid* of me. Twice.
My soft syllables rattle something
planted deep,
so I tell her to go where
she'd feel more comfortable
as if she were my niece or
godchild, even wish her
a good day.

If she stays, the ways
this could backfire!
Where is my Kevlar shield
from her shame?

There's no way to tell
when these breasts will evoke
solace or terror. I hate
that she surprises me, that I lull
myself to think her ilk
is gone despite knowing
so much more, and better.

I can't proselytize my worth
all semester, exhaust us
for the greater good.
I can't let her make me
a monster to myself—
I'm running out of time & pity
the extent of her impoverished
heart. She's from New
England; I'm from the Mid-South.
Far from elderly, someone
just raised her like this
with love.

I have essays to grade
but words warp
on the white page, dart
just out of reach. I blink
two hours away, find it hard
to lift my legs, my voice,
my head precious to my parents
now being held
in my own hands.

How did they survive
so much worse, the millions
with all of their scars!
What would these rivers be
without their weeping,
these streets without
their faith & sweat?

Fannie Lou Hamer
thundered what they felt,
we feel, into DNC microphones
on black and white TV
years before
I was a notion.

She doesn't know who
Fannie Lou Hamer is,
and never has to.

Kamilah Aisha Moon
Shared Plight

Bound to whims,
bred solely for
circuses of desire.
To hell with savannahs,
towns like Rosewood.

Domestics or domesticated,
one name or surnamed, creatures
the dominant ones can't live without
would truly flourish
without such devious love,
golden corrals.

Harnessed. Muzzled.
Stocks and bonds. Chains
and whips held by hand.
Ota Benga in a Bronx cage,
Saartjie Baartman on display—
funds sent to her village
didn't make it okay. Harambe,
Tamir, Cecil, Freddie—names
of the hunted, captives
bleed together. The captors
beasts to all but themselves
and their own.

Two endangered beings in a moat
stare into each other's eyes.

Slower than light, mercy
must not survive entry
into our atmosphere, never
reaching those who lose
unbridled lives
long before they die

in this world of zoos
and conquerors who treat
earthlings like aliens.

David Mura
Why Bruce Lee Is Sad

Can a fish be depressed? This question has been floating around my head ever since I spent a night in a hotel across from an excruciatingly sad-looking Siamese fighting fish. His name was Bruce Lee, according to a sign beneath his little bowl. . . . Bruce Lee, totally still, his lower fin grazing the clear faux rocks on the bottom of his home. When he did finally move, just slightly, I got the sense that he would prefer to be dead. . . . Was I simply anthropomorphizing Bruce Lee, incorrectly assuming his lethargy was a sign of mental distress?

—Heather Murphy, *New York Times*

because no one listens to fish
because I could have swum in the deepest oceans and coldest depths
because I swam the deepest oceans and coldest depths

because I pitched a show with a martial arts master wandering the West
because I could have torn apart David Carradine with one hand, blindfolded
because David Carradine stole my *Kung Fu*

because fish is a metaphor
and you in your bubble are watching me in my bubble
an inscrutable alien for your denigration and delight

because I wore a mask on *Green Lantern* when I took off my mask
because Kato chauffeured Britt Reid and did his master's bidding
because I could've kicked Van Williams's ass blindfolded with both hands tied

because the melancholy of fish is of far more interest
than the suicide rate of Asian American women
or depression in our men

because I didn't hear the cheers in Harlem when I thrashed Chuck Norris
because no one saw how much I held back to make the fight seem even
because Chuck Norris now stumps for Trump

because my white wife's family disowned her
because the martial arts world forbade my teaching *lo fahn* or blacks
because they bulleted my son Brandon on the set of *The Crow*

because a fish cannot choose its colors nor its name
because yellow is what they call a coward
because the fight in a fish can't be measured by its size

because when I swam back to Hong Kong no one noticed
because when I said, *Be water, my friend*
this aquarium wasn't my dream

because death stared from a thousand mirrors
and no fist could smash all that glass ceiling
because if you enter a dragon and come out a fish

you're surely a gook in America
where David Carradine—cursed
and self-asphyxiated in a sexual ritual—

isn't as sick as Chuck Norris
who once called me friend
braying for a man who would ban me

back to China to be stuffed in a fishbowl
looking as sad
as this world has become

David Mura
Minneapolis Public

There are 150 first languages in our schools
and so many aliens even E.T. would go unnoticed,
though if your tongue moved one way in the land of your birth
it must move another now, awkward at first.

There are blacks here who've never been to Africa;
Africans who've never heard a Baptist prayer,
much less the solemn dirges of Lutherans
or how the artist formerly known is some sort of Prince.

In the anthology of American Buddhist poetry
you will find not one face of a Tibetan
but they are here with girls and boys named Tenzin
and one, my son's good friend, throws a hard mean spiral.

Esmir is not the name of a girl but a Bosnian
boy who crouches at a table and glues a lamp together
and later with my other son conspires on a book—"A Touch
of Rabies"—a heartbreaking tale of good dogs gone bad.

(Why tell a soul of the sieges that brought him here
or stories of the Dali Lama or the temples destroyed
or troops of the warlords in the streets of Somalia,
the borders dividing death from safety if not evil and good?)

Say you're Egyptian or Haitian: Here you're singular,
not part of a Big Apple ghetto. If you're Chinese,
most likely you're adopted, or else your parents study
engineering at the U. And have I mentioned the Mexicans?

In *West Side Story* the rumble starts with Puerto Ricans
and working-class whites in a high school gym;
this year Maria's still Natalie Wood white to Jamaica's
half-black Anita, and the Jets sport blacks, one Tibetan,

and my hapa daughter who still doesn't question
such casting, or why *Bye Bye Birdie* last year

just might not be the choice of half the school
for a song and dance they could take on as their own.

Still, at the spring school dance J-Lo and Ja Rule
set the awkward bump and grind of junior high girls,
and the boys watch on the sidelines as boys that age do,
whether Bosnian, black, white, Somali, Tibetan.

I'm told we live in the Land of Great Lake Wobegon,
where all the women are strong, the men good-looking,
and the children above-average—and, I always add,
everyone's white. Hey, Tenzin, Nabil, go tell Garrison:

Not now. Not quite.

John Murillo
Upon Reading That Eric Dolphy Transcribed
Even the Calls of Certain Species of Birds,

I think first of two sparrows I met when walking home,
late night years ago, in another city, not unlike this—the one

bird frantic, attacking I thought, the way she swooped
down, circled my head, and flailed her wings in my face;

how she seemed to scream each time I swung; how she
dashed back and forth between me and a blood-red Corolla

parked near the opposite curb; how, finally, I understood:
I spied another bird, also calling, his foot inexplicably

caught in the car's closed door, beating his whole bird
body against it. Trying, it appeared, to bang himself free.

And who knows how long he'd been there, flailing. Who
knows—he and the other I mistook, at first, for a bat.

They called to me—something between squawk and chirp,
something between song and prayer—to do something,

anything. And, like any good god, I disappeared. Not
indifferent, exactly. But with things to do. And, most likely,

on my way home from another heartbreak. Call it 1997,
and say I'm several thousand miles from home. By which

I mean those were the days I made of everyone a love song.
By which I mean I was lonely and unrequited. But that's

not quite it either. Truth is, I did manage to find a few
to love me, but couldn't always love them back. The Rasta

law professor. The firefighter's wife. The burlesque dancer
whose daughter blackened drawings with m's to mean

the sky was full of birds the day her daddy died. I think
his widow said he drowned one morning on a fishing trip.

Anyway, I'm digressing. But if you asked that night—
did I mention it was night?—why I didn't even try

to jimmy the lock to spring the sparrow, I couldn't say,
truthfully, that it had anything to do with envy, with wanting

a woman to plead as deeply for me as these sparrows did,
one for the other. No. I'd have said something, instead,

about the neighborhood itself, the car thief shot a block
and a half east the week before. Or about the men

I came across nights prior, sweat-slicked and shirtless,
grappling in the middle of the street, the larger one's chest

pressed to the back of the smaller, bruised and bleeding
both. I know you thought this was about birds,

but stay with me. I left them both in the street—
the same street where I'd leave the sparrows—the men

embracing and, for all one knows (especially one not
from around there), they could have been lovers—

the one whispering an old, old, tune into the ear
of the other—*Baby, baby, don't leave me this way.* I left

the men where I'd leave the sparrows and their song.
And as I walked away, I heard one of the men call to me,

please or *help* or *brother* or some such. And I didn't break
stride, not one bit. It's how I've learned to save myself.

Let me try this another way. Call it 1977. And say
I'm back west, South Central Los Angeles. My mother

and father at it again. But this time in the street,
broad daylight, and all the neighbors watching. One,

I think his name was Sonny, runs out from his duplex
to pull my father off. You see where I'm going with this.

My mother crying out, fragile as a sparrow. Sonny
fighting my father, fragile as a sparrow. And me,

years later, trying to get it all down. As much for you—
I'm saying—as for me. Sonny catches a left, lies flat

on his back, blood starting to pool and his own
wife wailing. My mother wailing, and traffic backed,

now, half a block. Horns, whistles, and soon sirens.
1977. Summer. And all the trees full of birds. Hundreds,

I swear. And since I'm the one writing it, I'll tell you
they were crying. Which brings me back to Dolphy

and his transcribing. The jazzman, I think, wanted only
to get it down pure. To get it down exact—the animal

wracking itself against a car's steel door, the animals
in the trees reporting, the animals we make of ourselves

and one another. Flailing, failing. Stay with me now.
Days after the dustup, my parents took me to the park.

And in this park was a pond, and in this pond were birds.
Not sparrows, but swans. And my father spread a blanket

and brought from a basket some apples and a paring knife.
Summertime. My mother wore sunglasses. And long sleeves.

My father, now sober, cursed himself for leaving the radio.
But my mother forgave him, and said, as she caressed

the back of his hand, that we could just listen to the swans.
And we listened. And I watched. Two birds coupling,

one beating its wings as it mounted the other. Summer,
1977. I listened. And watched. When my parents made love

late into that night, I covered my ears in the next room,
scanning the encyclopedia for swans. It meant nothing to me—

then, at least—but did you know the collective noun
for swans is a *lamentation*? And is a lamentation not

its own species of song? What a woman wails, punch-drunk
in the street? Or what a widow might sing, learning her man

was drowned by swans? A lamentation of them? Imagine
the capsized boat, the panicked man, struck about the eyes,

nose, and mouth each time he comes up for air. Imagine
the birds coasting away and the waters suddenly calm.

Either trumpet swans or mutes. The dead man's wife
running for help, crying to any who'd listen. A lamentation.

And a city busy saving itself. I'm digressing, sure. But
did you know that to digress means to stray from the flock?

When I left my parents' house, I never looked back. By which
I mean I made like a god and disappeared. As when I left

the sparrows. And the copulating swans. As when someday
I'll leave this city. Its every flailing, its every animal song.

John Murillo
On Confessionalism

Not sleepwalking, but waking still,
   with my hand on a gun, and the gun
in a mouth, and the mouth
   on the face of a man on his knees.
Autumn of '89, and I'm standing
   in a Section 8 apartment parking lot,
pistol cocked, and staring down
   at this man, then up into the mug
of an old woman staring, watering
   the single sad flower to the left
of her stoop, the flower also staring.
   My engine idling behind me, a slow
moaning bass line and the bark
   of a dead rapper nudging me on.
All to say, someone's brokenhearted.
   And this man with the gun in his mouth—
this man who, like me, is really little
   more than a boy—may or may not
have something to do with it.
   May or may not have said a thing
or two, betrayed a secret, say,
   that walked my love away. And why
not say it: She adored me. And I
   her. More than anyone, anything
in life, up to then, and then still,
   for two decades after. And, therefore,
went for broke. Blacked out and woke
   having gutted my piggy and pawned
all my gold to buy what a homeboy
   said was a Beretta. Blacked out
and woke, my hand on a gun, the gun
   in a mouth, a man, who was really
a boy, on his knees. And because
   I loved the girl, I actually paused
before I pulled the trigger—once,
   twice, three times—then panicked
not just because the gun jammed,

but because what if it hadn't,
because who did I almost become,
    there, that afternoon, in a Section 8
apartment parking lot, pistol cocked,
    with the sad flower staring, because
I knew the girl I loved—no matter
    how this all played out—would never
have me back. Day of damaged ammo,
    or grime that clogged the chamber.
Day of faulty rods, or springs come
    loose in my fist. Day nobody died,
so why not *hallelujah*? Say *amen* or
    thank you? My mother sang for years
of God, babes, and fools. My father,
    lymph node masses fading from
his X-rays, said surviving one thing
    means another comes and kills you.
He's dead, and so, I trust him. Dead,
    and so I'd wonder, years, about the work
I left undone—boy on his knees
    a man now, risen, and likely plotting
his long way back to me. Fuck it.
    I tucked my tool like the movie gangsters
do, and jumped back in my bucket.
    Cold enough day to make a young man
weep, afternoon when everything,
    or nothing, changed forever. The dead
rapper grunted, the bass line faded,
    my spirits whispered something
from the trees. I left then lost the pistol
    in a storm drain, somewhere between
that life and this. Left the pistol
    in a storm drain, but can't remember
ever wiping away the prints.

John Murillo
Dolores, Maybe.

I've never spoken to anyone about this. Until now, until you.

I slept once in a field beyond the riverbank,
a flock of nightjars watching over me.

That was the summer a farmer found his daughter
hanging in the hayloft, and wished, for the first time,
he had not touched her so.

I wish I could say we were close—the girl and I,
I mean—but I only knew her to wave hello,

and walked her, once, halfway up the road
before turning finally into my grandmother's yard.

This was Ontario, California. 1983.
Which is to say, there was no river.
And I wouldn't know a nightjar if it bit me.

But the girl was real. And the day they found her, that was real.

And the dress she wore, same as on our walk—
periwinkle, she called it; I called it blue,
blue with bright yellow flowers all over

—the dress and the flowers, they too were real.

And on our walk, I remember, we cut through the rail yard,
and came upon a dead coyote lying near the tracks.

A frail and dusty heap of regret, he was companion to no one.

We stared at him for some time, our shadows stretched long and covering the
    animal.
She said something I'd remember for years, about loneliness,

but have long forgotten, the way I've forgotten—
though I can see her face as if she were standing right here—her very name.

Let's call her *Dolores*, from *dolor*. Spanish for *anguish*.

And whatever the sky, however lovely that afternoon,
I remember mostly the wind,
how a breeze unraveled what was left of a braid,

and when I tried to brush from Dolores's brow
a few loose strands, how she flinched,
how she ran the rest of the way home,

how I never saw her after that,
except when they carried her from the barn—her periwinkle dress,
her blue legs and arms, and the fields
ablaze with daisies.

I spent the rest of that summer in the rail yard
with my dead coyote, watching trains loaded and leaving.

All summer long, I'd pelt him with stones.
All summer long, I'd use the stones to spell the girl's name—
Dolores, maybe—in the dirt.

All summer long, fire ants crawled over and between each letter—
her name, now, its own small town.

A season of heat and heavy rains washed my coyote to nothing.
Only teeth and a few stubborn bones

that refused, finally, to go down.

Weeks into autumn, someone found the father
hanged from the same groaning tie-beams,
the hayloft black with bottle flies.

But that was 1983. Ontario, California.
Which is to say, the bottle flies are dead. So, too, the ants.
And neither field nor barn is where I left it.

I've never spoken to anyone about this. Until now, until you.

I gathered a handful of my coyote's bones, his teeth,
and strung them all on fishing wire—
a talisman to ward off anguish. A talisman I hold out to you now.

Please. Come closer. Take this from my hand.

Maria Nazos
Waitress in a Small-Town Seaside Tavern

Maybe a surfboard hit her, you say.
Though folks whisper, *her man beats her,*
and there are no waves today.
Her eye is black and sealed like a shutter.

We've all heard, her man, he beats her.
Still, we look at her and then look away,
her eye is sealed like a shutter.
(There are no waves this week; the sea is calm today.)

We glance at her, then quickly look away
as evening darkens the grey-green sea.
Since the ocean is calm today,
we drink; she brings us two more whiskeys.

Evening falls across the sea.
She lowers the lights; now the bar's dark too,
she brings us another round of whiskeys.
Now her bruise looks less black, more blue,

with the lights lowered—the bar's dark too—
so we can hardly see the mark,
her bruise looks less black and more blue.
You say, *maybe it's a shadow; it's just dark.*

Now we can barely see her mark,
as her man sits down with their boy in a booth.
You say *see: it's a shadow*. Outside it's getting dark.
She sags across him; slips off one shoe.

The man sitting with their son in the booth
reaches over and strokes her face.
She meets his gaze, slips off her other shoe:
her body's stiff, as if stuck in an invisible embrace.

Her man sits with her son in the booth.
Maybe a surfboard hit her, you say, again, hopefully.
But I see she's stuck in an invisible embrace,
and there are no waves today.

Maria Nazos
Overheard Proselytizing Dreadlocked Man's Ghazal

America: you're a junkyard dog, barely housebroken. Rich owner shaking
his useless finger. You snarl, but your chains are golden and can't stop shaking.

Thermometers split open. Windows melt. God's taken up golf.
He's made so many deals with white men and can't stop shaking!

Folks with accents are shipped off like cheap spices. *You're in America,
speak English*, they tell us Jamaicans. My head's hopeless and can't stop shaking.

I watch these majesties, these purple mountain majestic skies.
I need a drink. The sky's purple here in Hoboken. I can't stop shaking.

My eyes bleed when they take in too much beauty. Even the sun
barely recognizes this world; it's awoken and can't stop shaking.

I see bodies like petals littering the streets, the fire extinguisher's glass,
store windows, your bones they're all broken and can't stop shaking.

Every time our president's mouth opens, he pukes a red carpet.
Talk is cheap, his tongue drips arcade tokens and can't stop shaking.

Orange monster! Highlighter man! You squeak through passages of lies!
Our lives are dice—in a casino you can't keep open—and can't stop shaking.

Last week sixty people were mowed down like bushes of roses: Blood
like blossoms, they're silenced like lips that have spoken and can't stop shaking.

Sinéad O'Connor's crying in a hotel down the block and barely
hanging on: even she's penniless and alone and can't stop shaking.

You say I'm crazy? Hendrix said life is crazy. Man, we were riding
a butterfly. Now the wings are stuck in mid-motion and can't stop shaking.

Drowned islands of frogs and debris, the winds keep pummeling them—
Here in this country? If your English is broken, they won't let you stop shaking.

Maria: you can't hear me? Stop playing a walk-on in white men's movies. You walk steady, but your body's frozen, I see you: you can't stop shaking.

Marilyn Nelson
Honor Guard

Lost in blue stillness, I ride on a wave
of cumulous daydreams. We stand at ease,
whiling away our wait. Some birds call dibs
from the bordering trees. I check my watch.
They're twenty minutes late: He must be loved.
Distant traffic. A breeze tickles the leaves.

Under the cloud scud, a rolling landscape
of white markers in perfectly spaced rows.
I'm brought back from surfing the sky's sea-face
by crunching wheels and the call to attention.
We perform as drilled, precisely synchronized,
the ritual of warriors laying a comrade to rest.

The hearse delivers the flag-draped coffin
into the strict ballet of our white-gloved hands.
The riflemen fire a perfectly timed salute.
As the bugle plays the twenty-four notes of "Taps,"
I glance at the brown knot of the next of kin:
probably parents, siblings, his pregnant wife.

Pvt. Joseph Gonzales, of Tucson, was nineteen.
A roadside explosive device. We fold his flag
slowly into a triangle of stars
which the sergeant presents, with the nation's gratitude,
to the stunned child-bride-widow. The older man
stares into space. The older woman moans
Dios mío, Dios mío, Dios mío, ay Dios mío.

Naomi Shihab Nye
Seeing His Face

for Jaffar, in Dubai

When you said, first thing picking me up
at the airport—If he wins, we will have to see his face,
hear his voice, that would be so bad for all of us—
it seemed remote possibility. Day before the election, 2016,
breathing relief—surely this could not happen.

Very next day, together we reeled.
Into the bright sky, driving to
a school, pummeled by morning news—
desperately you kept flicking radio stations
Arabic, English, Farsi, saying, I'm afraid
it just happened. How could it happen?

Later was the first time in my life a librarian
would say to me, What the fuck?
Small children gathering, notebooks, pencils,
how could I speak a word, now that my own country
took such a swerve? Girls in little dark uniform sweaters,
with buttons. Smiling up. Tell us where to begin.

Naomi Shihab Nye
Gate A-4

Wandering around the Albuquerque airport terminal, after learning my flight had been detained four hours, I heard an announcement: "If anyone in the vicinity of Gate A-4 understands any Arabic, please come to the gate immediately." Well—one pauses these days. Gate A-4 was my own gate. I went there. An older woman in full traditional Palestinian embroidered dress, just like my grandma wore, was crumpled to the floor, wailing loudly. "Help," said the flight agent. "Talk to her. What is her problem? We told her the flight was going to be late and she did this." I stooped to put my arm around the woman and spoke to her haltingly. "Shu dow-a, Shu-bid-uck Habibti? Stani schway, Min fadlick, Shu-bit-se-wee?" The minute she heard any words she knew, however poorly used, she stopped crying. She thought the flight had been canceled entirely. She needed to be in El Paso for major medical treatment the next day. I said, "You're fine, you'll get there, who is picking you up? Let's call him." We called her son, I spoke with him in English. I told him I would stay with his mother till we got on the plane and ride next to her.

She talked to him. Then we called her other sons just for fun. Then we called my dad and he and she spoke for a while in Arabic and found out of course they had ten shared friends. Then I thought just for the heck of it why not call some Palestinian poets I know and let them chat with her? This all took up about two hours. She was laughing a lot by then. Telling about her life, patting my knee, answering questions. She had pulled a sack of home-made maamoul cookies—little powdered-sugar crumbly mounds stuffed with dates and nuts—out of her bag and was offering them to all the women at the gate. To my amazement, not a single woman declined one. It was like a sacrament. The traveler from Argentina, the mom from California, the lovely woman from Laredo—we were all covered with the same powdered sugar. And smiling. There is no better cookie. And then the airline broke out free apple juice from huge coolers and two little girls from our flight ran around serving it and they were covered with powdered sugar too. And I noticed my new best friend—by now we were holding hands—had a potted plant poking out of her bag, some medicinal thing, with green furry leaves. Such an old-country traveling tradition. Always carry a plant. Always stay rooted to some-where. And I looked around that gate of late and weary ones and thought, this is the world I want to live in. The shared world. Not a single person in that gate—once the crying of confusion stopped—seemed apprehensive about any other person. They took the cookies. I wanted to hug all those other women too. This can still happen anywhere. Not everything is lost.

Cynthia Dewi Oka
Driving to York Prison in a Thunderbird

with a belly full of sausage, it's hard not to give thanks
for contradiction. I mean, this is not my Thunderbird,
I didn't pay for this perspiring cup of sweet iced coffee,
I have no sway over the greyness of October infecting
the miles of visible world it contains. But I do appreciate
speed, and somehow, whipping past cows in their somber
contemplation of the wet earth, their tails swatting at flies
which I guess could be the bovine manifestation of social
anxiety, makes me feel like a body beyond history's gambit.
We pass so many lumpy fields yet to be gleaned (meaning
my eyes could have bled from the monotony) and pastel-
colored homes spaced so far apart I can't help thinking, no
wonder folks in these parts voted for the orange psychopath
obsessed with building a wall, but for the most part, keep
our promise to act like this is one big adventure, a hurtling
away from, not toward, the consequences of powerlessness.
I'm in the passenger seat, and Henry, whose nephew will
be facing the judge today, is punching the pedal like a god-
damn Dr. Who while taking strategic bites of his croissant
so as not to get buttery flakes all over the red leather seat.
In between, he regales me with his early years in America
(he was a banker back home) scrubbing toilets in exchange
for a sushi chef apprenticeship. (He's a restaurateur now.)
I too, offer tales of sacrifice and survival, because well,
what else do you do while you are being hunted? The rain
paints its fleeting destinies on the car windows, and I think
of the common itineraries adventure takes: escape from
point A to point B, or, return, i.e., anywhere you go ends up
point A. There was one night, a long time ago, in a car
like this one but stolen, in another country, with the top off,
when I beat my chest like King Kong at the moon because
I couldn't scream with all that wind, a whole country of wind,
rushing down my throat. I was a runaway then, a dropout,
a fuck-up, and still I get nostalgic about the colors of those
days, lead and mulberry, how one chased the other, lightning
in my periphery when I threw my fists at the boys and the law.
They landed nowhere, and I'm not even mad, because escape

is the story we tell so we can live with the echoes of choices
we made in greed, hunger, pain. Right now, Henry is saying
that his daughters have no time for him, so, "I will treat you
like you are one of them." This isn't the first time I've been
a stand-in; it could be the closest thing we've invented to time
travel. He's standing in, too, for my dad, who would have never
driven a Thunderbird (he was the kind of guy who hit the brakes
every few seconds when there was no other car on the road. Plus
he was a dentist), or stopped at a gas station just to let me buy
a pack of cigarettes. At some point, I stop trying to find aesthetic
value in the cows' sad, lolling heads. Ahead of us, the prison
rises with its crown of barbed wire like solid blocks of rotten
milk out of the dead grasses. I've never been here, but I almost
cry with recognition. Of course. Of course. There is where I've
left my heart, in the box of metallic things you can't bring inside.
Henry parks his beautiful machine and we walk toward the blue
doors, naked without our gadgets, not touching but leaning toward
each other—he's my dad's height, shorter than me—in the dogged rain.

Brenda Marie Osbey
As Yet Untitled: A Seasonal Suite

it is that time of year when the killings increase
season of hate and violence puling entitlement of those with only pallor to trade
to stand behind before
sheets held up frayed through at center
making cross-eyes at the dark world beyond its own
small patch
and blood on the fields
seeped into and under the well- or poorly-paved sidewalks
highways littered with shells
campuses littered in candles
and the rant and rant and rant of what
echoing
the suddenly vacant streets

this nation hardly ever awake from long dullish sleep
nightmare reflections

it is any day date year month time
time doing time
hardest sun in a region without borders or bounds
all-inclusive all-enveloping explosion of hard daylight
and night somehow fails to encompass embrace condescend
fails to fall
unlike the bodies
humped spattered outlined heaping after-crime scenes of suburban cul-de-sacs
small city traffic lanes major metropolitan area thoroughfares rural mail routes
kindergartens gymnasiums waterfronts campuses churches driveways

era and epoch season absent reckoning absent succor
inclement both to shadow and to shade to twilight and to dusk
that time of year
inclement
to the gloaming
to nightfall

to the dark
to the black

no longer interval or spell neither span nor while nor stretch nor term but season
having evolved as do flora fauna land formations hurricanes
thundering up out of oceans across seas bearing
mitochondria of lynch mobs of men and of women of children mutating
quickly smoothly stealthily away
from implement drudge shifting swiftly morphing to
appliance shifting continually perceptibly imperceptibly to
bureaucracy industry post-industrial apparat service-oriented
slaughter

no longer trailing tracking trapping outriding
simple outright
close of day
sunset become
great sprawling map
single massive sundown town
unseasonable
unseasonable now eve eventide evening
night nightfall
gloaming
dusk to dark the shade the shine
to the black
to the dark to the
black
time of year

Alicia Ostriker
The Light (We all came from somewhere else)

What is the birthplace of the light that stabs me with joy
and what is the difference between avocados sold on the street
by a young man conceived in Delhi and avocados sold

in the West Side Market by cornrow girls, I am anyhow afloat
in tides of Puertorican, Cuban, Mexican, Westindian Spanish, wavelets of Urdu
swelling like oceans, sweating like jackhammers, rasping like crows, calling out

in the West Side Market, the Rite Aid, and every other shop on the street
Por qué no comprendes, you don't own this city any more
the city belongs and has always belonged to its shoals of exiles

crashing ashore in foaming salty droplets, *cómo no, gringita—*
with their dances and their grandmothers, with their drinking and their violence
and their burning yearning for dignity, and smelling money, what, what is the joy

is it those lamps of light those babies in their strollers
those avocados with their dark-green pebbled rinds, shining from inside
two for four dollars in the West Side Market, and three for four dollars from the cart

joy like white light between the dollar bills, is it these volleys of light fired
by ancestors who remember tenements, the sweatshops, the war,
who supposed their children's children would be rich and free?

Alicia Ostriker
Ghazal: America the Beautiful

Do you remember our earnestness our sincerity
in first grade when we learned to sing America

The Beautiful along with the Star-Spangled Banner
and say the Pledge of Allegiance to America

We put our hands over our first-grade hearts
we felt proud to be citizens of America

I said One Nation Invisible until corrected
maybe I was right about America

School days school days dear old Golden Rule Days
when we learned how to behave in America

What to wear, how to smoke, how to despise our parents
who didn't understand us or America

Only later learning *Banner* and *Beautiful*
live on opposite sides of the street in America

Only later discovering the Nation is divisible
by money by power by color by gender by sex America

We comprehend it now, this land is two lands
one triumphant bully one still hopeful America

Imagining amber waves of grain blowing in the wind
purple mountains and no homeless in America

Sometimes I still put my hand tenderly on my heart
somehow or other still carried away by America

Willie Perdomo
Brother Lo on the Prison Industrial Complex

Brother Lo was a story master, a library without a card, a *cuento*
    king who could drop fables bout the Young Lords, the
    spiritual values of Japanese swords, the degree of separation
    between concrete & rain, the melt of ice cream & pain.

He once said, *One hand can't wash the other if you're busy*
    counting with your fingers—

He also said, *The law is one top spin after another and bankrolls*
    beget death tolls.

This was before the two baddest buildings in the city were
    knocked out with a fuel-injected Guernica, before the
    city officials had a Jones for breaking book spines.

The so-called bar starts early, says Brother Lo.

Starts with a permission slip for a class trip to the local precinct.
Starts with *If you see something, you better not say shit.*
Your teacher will urge you to get excited.
Free mug shots if you behave.
You're going to get arrested like it was for real:
cheese sandwiches, sour milk, dented oranges,
& a hint of ammonia in your cough.

There will even be a contest to see how long you can stay
    handcuffed to a classmate before you decide to throw him
    under the bus.

Before you leave the school, your teacher will ask you to line up
    for a head count.

It should be fun, your teacher will say.

Trip day comes and you see your first chain gang, a head speed-
    bumped into a desktop, a door creaking to a close on a
    confession.

The bus ride home will be less park than amusement.

The sirens will sound petrified, but happy.

Your mother doesn't believe in conspiracies, so she's good
with it.

Your father was a revolutionary before he sold the revolution for
two bundles & a quarter water.

You can measure the bus ride back home by years.

When it's time to show & tell, the only thing you can remember
was standing on line, waiting for copies of your free mug
shots, and right before you left the precinct you heard the
desk sergeant taking bets that half the class will come back
arrested for real.

Emmy Pérez
Not one more refugee death

A river killed a man I loved,
And I love that river still
                                    —María Meléndez

1

Thousands of fish killed after Pemex
spill in el Río Salado and everyone
runs out to buy more bottled water.
Here in El Valle, the Río Grande kills
crossers as does the sun, like the heat

of Arizona and the ranchlands around
the Falfurrias checkpoint. It's hard
to imagine an endangered river
with that much water, especially
in summer and with the Falcon Reservoir

in drought, though it only takes inches
to drown. Sometimes, further west,
there's too little river
to paddle in Boquillas Canyon
where there are no steel-column walls

except the limestone canyon's drop
and where a puma might push-wade across,
or in El Paso, where double-fenced muros
sparkle and blind with bullfight ring lights,
the ring the concrete river mold, and above

a Juárez mountain urges
La Biblia es La Verdad—Leela.

2

Today at the vigil, the native singer
said we are all connected
by water, la sangre de vida.

Today, our vigil signs proclaimed
McAllen is not Murrieta.
#iamborderless. Derechos
Inmigrantes=Derechos
Humanos. Bienvenidos niños.
We stand with refugee children.
We are all human. Bienvenidos
a los Estados Unidos.

And the songs we sang
the copal that burned
and the rose petals spread
en los cuatro puntos were
for the children and women
and men. Songs

for the Guatemalan
boy with an Elvis belt buckle
and Angry Birds jeans with zippers
on back pockets who was found
shirtless in La Joya, one mile
from the river. The worn jeans

that helped identify his body
in the news more times
than a photo of him while alive.
(I never knew why the birds
are angry. My mother said
someone stole their eggs.)

The Tejas sun took a boy
I do not know, a young man
who wanted to reach Chicago,
his brother's number etched in
his belt, his mother's pleas not
to leave in white rosary beads

he carried. The sun in Tejas
stopped a boy the river held.
Detention centers filled, churches
offer showers and fresh clothes.

Water and a covered porch may
have waited at a stranger's house

or in a patrol truck had his body
not collapsed. Half of our bodies
are made of water, and we can't
sponge rivers through skin
and release them again
like rain clouds. Today

at the vigil the native singer
sang we are all connected
by water, la sangre de vida.

Marge Piercy
Illegal with Only Hope

The mother imagines [a few more
steps, another push across a mine-
field, just one more night hiding
in rank bushes] she can carry

her child across the border
to some kind of safety, anything
better than what she flees, hauling
her child though the fields of hell.

She has a wound on her leg
untended, unbandaged, bleeding
now and then when weeds, branches
brush it. She has a deep wound

inside: the wan face of her older child
as the life drained from it with
blood from the blast that tore
his flesh apart. The dusty body

of her husband fallen into a ditch—
the ditch where she huddled holding
tight the still living child who is all
she can imagine of any future.

So she slugs forward toward
that invisible border where mothers
can keep their children safe,
perhaps, in a world on fire.

Marge Piercy
Way Late December 2016

A cold rain pushes in on the wind
dashing sideways into my eyes
and hair. A lone gull is blown
almost inside out like an umbrella

his wings outspread. He dives
to a roof and settles, still ruffled
and spiky. The bare trees bend.
The oaks' tough leaves tear loose.

It's close enough to the shortest
day that it never feels quite light.
This is the butt end of the year.
It's hard to celebrate what's coming:

hard times for those of us not rich.
Times when the overlords gloat
and I search for something good
like a pig rooting in sour mud.

The news of the day is grey and dark;
it explodes shards into my ears,
my eyes. Danger rides the wind
like ash and chokes me as I breathe.

Sasha Pimentel
For Want of Water

an ant will drown himself, his body submerging into ease, his mandibles,
       head, antennae, baptized. How lovely

to lose your senses to the cup of your want. A boy drags his mother's body
       across the desert, her fluids rising

to god in order to quench her skin. How divine her body must have looked,
       clutched at the ankles, her

arms reaching out in exultation, her head stippled in rings of sand and blood
       as he walked with her, slowly, her fallen

and moving shape the fork of a divining rod, her body shaking with each of his
       steps, and for water, shaking to find

that deep and secret tributary. I have dreams of letting go of water, of waking
       my lover to a bed of my urine

as my brother did to me, his thin limbs shaking to discover the shame of his
       inside self. And what did we know that to have

an inside wet enough to free was luxury? The boy walks with his mother—he
       is only thirteen—the age I learned

to stroke on the toilet the blood off my fingers, and he cannot cry, because to
       cry would mean the waste of his own

wetness, to cry would mean to stop, to think, to differentiate the liquids
       moving down his face, to cry would mean

to cry, so he goes on, and—this is a common story, the boy is not a boy now
       but every boy we have ever known—people

find him, they help him to lift his mother onto their hands, their necks, they
       lift her to their own dark and desperate

dryness, and they make it, yes, when they make it over the border to a mall
        parking lot, they lay her down, they fall with her

body as a clump of bodies behind a city dumpster, and people make calls from
        behind windows, not

to the immigrants with the dying core, but to the police, who come with their
        handcuffs and call her *dead*. No. To call

would be to give her life a name. Roundness to where there are now only
        angles. To call would be to remember all

the other times that he has called for her, and the boy plugs his ears, shakes his
        head, doesn't know that he cannot physically

produce tears anymore—such thirst can rid us of these symbols—only that
        now there are mouths around him calling other names

as men run and other men give chase, because how much do you need to give
        up in order to stay? a boy? a mother? your land and inner

land? Nothing. Nothing can be given, and he will remember nothing as he sits
        in a cell waiting for his sister to come to release

him from his cellular pain. He will only remember water, that want for the
        clouds to let go their rain, and how seeing

them dropping, he kept pulling forward, their bodies steady towards that
        dark, uneven line.

Robert Pinsky
From An Explanation of America

Serpent Knowledge

. . . As in the universal provincial myth
That sees, in every stranger, a mad attacker . . .
(And in one's victims, it may be, a stranger).
Strangers—the Foreign who, coupling with their cousins
Or with their livestock, or even with wild beasts,
Spawn children with tails, or claws and spotted fur,
Ugly—and though their daughters are beautiful
Seen dancing from the front, behind their backs
Or underneath their garments are the tails
Of reptiles, or teeth of bears.

                        So one might feel—
Thinking about the people who cross the mountains
And oceans of the earth with separate legends,
To die inside the squalor of sod huts,
Shanties, or tenements; and leave behind
Their legends, or the legend of themselves,
Broken and mended by the generations:
Their alien, orphaned, and disconsolate spooks,
Earth-trolls or Kallikaks or Snopes or golems,
Descended of Hessians, runaway slaves and Indians,
Legends confused and loose on the roads at night . . .
The Alien or Creature of the movies.
As people die, their monsters grow more tame;
So that the people who survived Saguntum,
Or in the towns that saw the Thirty Years' War,
Must have felt that the wash of blood and horror
Changed something, inside. Perhaps they came to see
The state or empire as a kind of Whale
Or Serpent, in whose body they must live—
Not that mere suffering could make us wiser,
Or nobler, but only older, and more ourselves. . . .
On television, I used to see, each week,
Americans descending in machines
With wasted bravery and blood; to spread

Pain and vast fires amid a foreign place,
Among the strangers to whom we were new—
Americans: a spook or golem, there.
I think it made our country older, forever.
I don't mean better or not better, but merely
As though a person should come to a certain place
And have his hair turn gray, that very night.

Gabriel Ramírez
If Pit Bulls Had a Justice System It'd Be Belly Rubs

not the needles. no lethal injection.
not hung. no noose. no rope whatsoever.
not starved. wearing bones like a wedding dress.
get it through your thick skull. not the bullets.
breed-specific legislation sounds like
one-drop rule. you Pit Bull. you too killed cruel.
without fair trial. gotta get put down.
because your size. because all them lied.
because they afraid and would rather you
this way. in your unmarked grave. you're to blame
for being born this banned breed of loyal.
February 13, 2016.
Spike. four-year-old blue nose. shot in the head
by cop for wagging his tail in the Bronx.

Gabriel Ramírez
Cotto the Pit Bull of Borinquén

When we felt the first wind of Maria
Cotto raised his head from the toilet and
was called to greater water. With purpose
in his paws. Cotto stood at the edge of
Borinquén and barked as the tide would rise.
Cotto chiseled. Cotto got a good song
in his blood about not dying. Cotto
submerged and Cotto kept barking. Cotto
kept barking. Cotto kept barking. Cotto
barked till his blood-song split the clo/uds. Cotto
brought light back to Borinquén like bones thrown
from a deity's hand. Cotto returned
home. Lowered his head into the toilet.
There wasn't any water. Still isn't.

Luivette Resto
Breakfast Conversation with My Oldest Son

Another man shot today, mom.
I don't think I ever want a license.

Driving isn't the problem, mijo.
Driving isn't the problem.

Luivette Resto
A Poem for the Man Who Asked Me:
Where Are Your Motherhood Poems?

He didn't have the predictable inquiries
do I write in Spanish more than English
do I italicize the Spanish words
or include a translation glossary at the back of the book

with an accusatory tone like a private investigator
out to solve the case of the missing poems
as if I purposely erased my kids' existence and memories
in some poetic version of witness protection

should I write more about the irony of never wanting to be a mother in the
    first place
while other girls talked about having babies and a husband after college
I spoke about wanting eighty-hour work weeks
burying myself in depositions

should I write more about the abortion I had at twenty-two
find the appropriate simile for the feel of the vacuum in my cervix
how I made my future husband witness and hold my hand
while I sobbed on the exam table legs wide open
reminding me how I got there in the first place

I think about the women who cannot have children
the price tag of IVF the bureaucracy of adoption
the women who still have to prove to their tías mothers
sisters other women that their worth isn't in the uterus

because my body's sole purpose
is to be a vessel of life and not sexual satisfaction
never contemplating the perfect metaphor for the best orgasm I ever had

I should be careful of slut-shaming myself in my sonnets
when I say fucking versus making love
pussy versus vagina
dick versus manhood

so where are the mother poems in question
they are embedded here
in the pores and cells
of this poem that cannot wait to breathe

Peggy Robles-Alvarado
At Every Family Party Where the Grown-Ups Drank Too Much

We knew we inherited these mouths.
Forced openings of treacherous scowls,
all crooked-toothed and salivating,
descendants of Caribs, dressed in pink tulle and lace.
Too much lip, too much tongue to keep quiet.
Too much bite to let them run their dirty fingers over our
half-smiles, knowing drunk uncles weren't just wiping off our
little girl grins, they wanted us dirty—
wanted to choke out the pulsing of war-cry pressing at our
underdeveloped chests, wanted to reteach our jaws to
open wide in surrender. But we: daughters of savages,
surnamed chaos, learned to dance for Guabancex before
they baptized her María. We: spat rituals of rupture into
their half-finished Solo cups, trying to reverse
the root, unwilling to justify the ache—
We: the niñas bonitas pero malcriadas, renamed what they
wanted to call silence—explosive.

Luis J. Rodríguez
Heavy Blue Veins: Watts, 1959

Heavy blue veins streak across my mother's legs,
Some of them bunched up into dark lumps at her ankles.
Mama periodically bleeds them to relieve the pain.
She carefully cuts the engorged veins with a razor
And drains them into a porcelain-like metal pail
Called a *tina*.
I'm small and all I remember are dreams of blood,
Me drowning in a red sea, blood on sheets, on the walls,
Splashing against the white pail in streams
Out of my mother's ankle.
But they aren't dreams.
It is Mama bleeding—into day, into night.
Bleeding a birth of memory: my mother, my blood,
By the side of the bed, me on the covers,
And her slicing into a black vein
And filling the pail into some dark, forbidding
Red nightmare, which never stops coming,
Nevers stops pouring,
This memory of Mama and blood and Watts.

William Pitt Root
The Mill of Grief

after Sabahud-Deen Kraidi (Arabic, 1936–)

The Mill of Grief creaks and turns, turns,
scattering ash in the countenance of Heaven,
burying the fields, clogging nostrils,
interring every blossom, supplanting air.

Each sunrise it assigns its crew
to gather bones in great baskets—
bones from the grave's core, cavern bones,
bones pried from the eagle's talons.

All night it creaks and turns, turns,
all day it creaks and turns,
rendering to ash these bones God made,
creaking, "No rebirth, no life hereafter!"

When the moon ascends it shudders,
when the moon declines it laughs.
Turning youth into age it creaks,
turning spring into fall it groans.

Each night the ash piles higher.
Hungry thieves who steal the flour
bake their loaves, build highways, bridges,
spanning wastes from hell to hell.

More ashes! More bones!
And the Mill creaks and turns.

William Pitt Root
White Boots: Ghost of the San Manuel Mine

for James G. Davis

As you know, Jim, I did work underground
in the same mine you've imagined
    in your studio: half a mile down, taking
wages enough to make it to California
and fool's gold enough to remind me
    I don't know much after all.

New guys like myself—still thrilled
by the dangers of fire or falling
    through the dark into a hole followed
by twenty tons of dusty rumbling ore—
we all tried to stay alert
    each minute of the eight-hour shift.

And for a week or two, alert we were,
then habit made us careless as the rest
    so we'd pocket our safety glasses,
let dust masks dangle from our necks,
and sometimes catch each other
    stepping out across open shafts

without first snapping our lanyards
to the rusty cables overhead.
    The buddy system wasn't much observed,
so like the rest come break time
I'd kick back alone against the stone wall
    and light up, flicking my headlamp off

so the dark expanded, flooding gently
through my eyes. In the distance,
    sometimes, a solitary hunched figure
projecting its small wedge of light
would glide by my line's entrance
    tiny as a fly in a tear of amber

from where I watched, invisible
and isolate as a stone in outer space,
    or inner space. Just some guy.

Never saw old White Boots in those days
but often thought how all those men
    just lost in the Sunshine Mine
must have felt—poor bastards
who lived long enough to feel,
    long enough to lose everything
in their minds but hope
before their air was gone, long after
    their light. You'd have to kill your light

to keep from igniting whatever gases
might be seeping from walls,
    so dark is where you'd be,
whether by yourself or in the company of others.
In such a dark I had no need of White Boots, my friend,
    but looking at this image, startling, almost comic,

you've drawn from the dark of blinding inks
and your own heart familiar with disaster,
    I'm reminded now of how it is
the living keep hold of the things
that bind them to those gone—
    how Gypsies, when a loved one's dying,

will help the one failing stay just a little longer
by turning a wooden chair upside down
    to hold between them. On one leg
a live hand, the dying on another,
until, ready, it falls free. But
    the thing is the clasp itself

across that final distance,
how it allows those last things
    that need saying to be said.
That's how it's always seemed
    to me, with art I mean. Whether
    it's paint on canvas or ink on a page,

it's the chance for what knows it must die in us
to join what knows it will live forever.
    And knowledge from such a common depth
only survives in the light as shadow,
as White Boots, *imago*, as a way, meanwhile,
    to stay in touch while the sun burns on.

Patrick Rosal
At the Tribunals

Once, in a brawl on Orchard I clocked a kid
with a ridgehand so hard I could feel

his top teeth give. His knees buckled
and my homeboy let loose a one-two

to finish the job. I turned around
to block a sucker punch that didn't come.

We ducked under the cops' bright red
hatchets that swung around the corner.

I never saw the first kid drop. He must
have been still falling when I dipped

from the scene and trotted toward
Delancey. He was falling when I stopped

to check my leather for scuff marks.
He was falling when I slipped inside

a dive to hide from a girl who got ghost
for books. He was falling when I kissed

the Santo Niño's white feet and Melanie's
left collarbone and the forehead

of one punk whose nose I busted
for nothing but squaring off with me,

his head snapped back to show his neck's
smooth pelt. Look away long enough

and a boy can fall for weeks—decades—
even as you get down on one knee

to pray the rotting kidneys in your mom's
gut don't turn too quick to stone.

I didn't stick around to watch
my own work. I didn't wait for

a single body to hit the pavement.
In those days, it was always spring

and I was mostly made of knives.
I rolled twenty-two deep, every

one of us lulled by a blade
though few of us knew the steel note

that chimed a full measure if you slid
the edge along a round to make it

keen. I'll tell those stiffs in frocks
to go ahead and count me among

the ones who made nothing good
with his bare hands. I'll confess,

I loved the wreckage: no matter
the country, no matter the machine.

Joseph Ross
For Zella Ziona

in memory of Zella Ziona, transgender twenty-one-year-old,
murdered October 15, 2015, in Gaithersburg, Maryland

Because the reasons
he shot you in an alley

are not reasons. Because
he thinks you embarrassed him

in front of men.
Because these men speak

a language unknown
in your shifting world.

Because "also known as"
is a funeral in America.

Because "gunshot wounds
to the head and groin"

speak clearly a language
some men know.

Because when a Black girl
is called a Black boy

by a maternity nurse,
the language dissolves again,

the name crumbles and a soul
must wait to emerge.

Because she might be born again,
not of Jesus but of herself.

Because you took your own name,
baptized in your own language,

named for a saint only you pray to.
Because your saint does not

stop bullets just because
you are beautiful.

Nicholas Samaras
All Extinction Is Gradual at First

First, we noticed the trees
beginning to leave us—
shedding their cowls earlier in summer.

We thought: an off season.
But the same thing happened the next year, too.
Then, the days of spring grew impossibly thin—

we morphed from winters that wouldn't leave us
to the swelter of summers in staccato.
No season behaved itself.

Weather became a wild animal biting
anything in its path.
We don't think about the last time

we saw bees swarming around.
We don't see abundance the way we used to
and only the endangered lists grow longer.

These mornings, I look out onto a browning world
growing chiller faster, while thinking, *elephant, tiger.*
I move to tell my children about them.

Ruth Irupé Sanabria
Ars Poetica

Story takes her skin. Story takes her bones.
She finds her toes and her fingertips.
When she speaks, like salmon running,
the dead and the living converge.
The river of memory rocks
the hunger of claws and tongues.
Electricity swallows itself back
through its double-prod *picana*,
bullets dislodge themselves from
their chore of destroying
the same day over and over again,
and from the caverns of fear and revision,
skin resurrects the skin.
Each sentence closes in
like the crawl of split skin
sealing its red, wet avulsion.

The enormity of the pending night scares the seven assassins on trial.
They understand that in hell, they will eat their own throats.

Ruth Irupé Sanabria
A Tree in Perth Amboy

last spring,
they cut off 3 arms,
left her two.

this spring,
two arms bloom
at dawn, full green.

now, they saw her two arms
then shave her—
a living stump between cement.

the birds, 300 spring birds,
trill at the emergency. my plants stiffen
at attention, i close the windows,
but they angle their main leaves
and hear the sound.

now, a pale umber oblong stick
hits her first and final beat,
but there is no leather,
copper, or even some earth
to receive her death song,
only cement street.
her death weight is heavy.
her sound, the hollow sound
of drum with no skin.

my house shakes,
my sofa shakes,
i shake. she is gone,
she is fed into the grinder,
the birds are silent.

Lauren Marie Schmidt
The Social Worker's Advice

The Haven House for Homeless Women and Children

Jabbing a finger at my face, you say, *You can't have
empathy. Empathy will eat you alive*, as if empathy
were a beast with feathers, fur, and hair, with hind legs
and deft feet, wings and claws, a beast that soars,
stalks, lunges, springs, a beast that chases, a beast
that screams instead of sings, with giant jaws
and a tongue budded with a rapacious taste for fools
like me, fools who don't believe the beast exists to eat,
who let it burrow its snout between our legs, fingers,
up to our armpits—the spaces of our common human stink.

But you see a beast that sniffs and snarls for a thick blue vein
to sic, and when I look at you I understand the beast more plainly—
I see that its skin collects pock marks each time you dock
merit points to teach the mothers not to "talk Black,"
I see that its forehead sprouts a thousand of your scornful eyes,
its claws slash as swift and deep as your condescension—

because what you mean is that I can't have empathy
for these girls, for times like these, for a place like this,
for Nicole who tallies the number of days it's been
since she last flushed her veins with a spoon-cooked mix,
twenty-eight days and counting. No empathy
for Nicole because she can never seem to find
matching socks for her four-year-old son, or because
she folds flowers from twice-used computer paper
to calm her nerves. Bouquets of paper daisies
sprout from vases on all four tables in the dining room.

What you mean is that I can't have empathy for Takina,
who was told to go by Tina because her white, adoptive
mother—middle-aged, middle-classed—prefers it.
Her birth-mother is five years gone and Tina-Takina
thinks she might be pregnant again. I can't have empathy

for Denice who is pregnant with her third, but didn't know
until she was too far in, for Angelica who fell down the stairs
while holding her infant son, too spent from pre-sun
feedings and weeping in the wee hours as the minutes lurch by.
Each tick-tock is the sound of the dead-locked door
of the nighttime aide who snores in the small room
near the exit like a beast at the gates, preventing escape
from this place, this time, from lives like these
without signing a release form for the Division of Youth
and Family Services, like Dionna, who took her two kids
to a hotel where, alone, at night, she stares at ceiling holes
in the red glow of the word VACANCY flashing through
windows with no curtains. I can't have empathy for LaQuita,
so thin that when she aims her breast at her baby's lips,
she prays she has something wet and real to give.

When you say, with your wagging finger, *You can't have
empathy. Empathy will eat you alive*, what you mean
is that I can't have empathy for these girls, and when I look
at you, I cannot help but wonder when you first believed
empathy would do more than sniff and lick your palms.

So I say, let it take me, then, this beast of your invention,
let it slip its fangs into my skin and tear through my throat,
let it suck all the fat and blood from off my solid bones.

Tim Seibles

Lucky

after the mass killing at the Pulse nightclub in Orlando, Florida

Rain falls into the open eyes of the dead
Again again with its pointless sound

Once:
I thought I knew how to read
this   but I have
fooled myself, afraid to see
this blind lobby, this bad
dream, this thanatocracy that
runs my country. I remain

astonished
by a certain calculated
ignorance—
in spite of all the grief,
in spite of all the
marches: the idea that
brown skin   is a reason
to stop a life.

So, it remains
hard to be black
here—and, of course, hard
to be female or poor
or "queer"—whatever
your complexion. Will it
take much

longer? How long
before we know each execution,
each exit wound
prints the lost blood
on all of us:

each of us often
alone   opening a door, hoping
to dance with someone
who, for a moment, sees
only the promise of rhythm
holding our faces.

This morning, fresh light
opened your eyes
and told you
that *this* is what
eyes do: show the world

no matter what,
no matter how much
we don't want to see
how life   breaks in,
breaks a day that seemed
like other days: a Monday
when you ran errands
slightly annoyed
by the price of food.

Then   the TV voices—

adding up "the casualties,"
sorry for "conflicting
reports," wondering
what the _____ community
is feeling   *given such
terror, given such a
terrible thing,* given
this systemic insanity
packaged and delivered
as if by secret courier.

I have been close
to some killings,
not many. When that shooter
held the bell tower in Texas,

I was a boy in a city up north,
where boys like me
joined gangs to bleed
each other   and now

in Florida, *this*—with me, a grown-up
in Virginia   and a year ago, nine
black folks shot in their church
by some sick-fuck supremacist,
and yesterday another brotha
murdered by a badge
in Minnesota, Louisiana, Illinois—
this is not *bad news*: this
is America   rubbing your eyes,
lighting your whole day with death:

and you might believe
that you were
blessed

not to have been *there*,

not to have your missing face
taped to a wall, not to "know

any
of the people
who died"—

but that's what
I mean, that's what I'm

trying to talk about: this daze,
this near intoxication, this

feeling *lucky*

that the blood on TV
isn't yours, that you're

alright—again,
that it isn't
you   again

who's dying

Epigraph is from W. S. Merwin, "The Asians Dying"

Katherine DiBella Seluja
Letter to My Suegra, from Artesia, New Mexico

it's easier to cross the babies one at a time
on inner tubes or rafts,
that way, I notice if one goes under.

—Anonymous coyote

Querida suegra, they're holding Dora and the children in jail, Dora
and so many children. Children who've traveled north
in the shadows and trusted coyotes to be their guides.

You remember Dora, don't you, *suegra*? The little brown girl with
the pet monkey named Boots. The girl who says *lo hicimos* and
unodostres. Her face everywhere here, on sneakers, on Band-
Aids, on bathing suits and water bottles. And now behind
barbed wire fences, nine feet high.

Nothing like *el muro* on Tiburcio Gómez all the *sobrinos* loved so
much. They'd lean on the wall in the evening, waiting for Don
Lorenzo to turn out the light. Gustavo and Alvaro would climb *la
parra*, reaching for the sweetest, darkest grapes. Stretching out
so far they almost brought the whole *viña* down. Their penance,
rinsing fruit for days, while Don Lorenzo's sons crushed *las uvas*
beneath their feet.

No grapes here for the children to cram their mouths full. No
sneakers or water bottles for these children brought to the banks
of the Río Grande, told to swim right to the uniformed men.
Thrashing their arms, flapping their mud-stained feet.

Don Share
From Crown Decline

We, at the height, are ready to decline.
—Shakespeare, *Julius Caesar*

*

Dreamers, we called them. But who
Elected you to shift dream into nightmare?
Who made humanity a dream, and who?
Dreamers, we called them. Who
Enacted this question of legality? Who?
When we are born, we each must fare . . .
Dreamers, we called them. But who
Elected you to shift dream into nightmare?

*

A monument is not history.
History is not a monument.
A statue is not liberty.
A monument is not history.
There's no epiphany in bigotry.
History is not heaven-sent.
A monument is not history.
History is not a monument.

*

Robert E. Lee, still in bronze—
Will you surrender again?
Dismount, Sir, for the Union.
[Here insert emoticons]

Uncivil wars: if you're not
With me, you're antifa me.
No one leads in effigy.
Let these crowds part, and depart.

*

All the new thinking is un-
Like the old thinking: That is
Because it appears that our
Brains are melting like glaciers.

*

The farther away in time
I get from my late father
The more interesting he gets
Founding Fathers: not so much

*

You have to walk slow
In dreams so nobody sees
You; the great fires are
No longer in our souls but
Outside us altogether.

Danez Smith
sometimes i wish i felt the side effects

but there is no proof but proof
no mark but the good news

there is no bad news yet. again.
i wish i knew the nausea, its thick yell

in the morning, pregnant proof
that in you, life swells. i know

i'm not a mother, but i know what it is
to nurse a thing you want to kill

& can't. you learn to love it. yes.
i love my sweet virus. it is my proof

of life, my toxic angel, wasted utopia
what makes my blood my blood.

i get it now, how beauty so loved
her warden. you stare at fangs

long enough, even fangs pink
with your own blood look soft.

//

low key, later, it felt like i got it
out the way, to finally know it

up close, see it in the mirror.
it doesn't feel good to say.

it doesn't feel good to know
your need outweighed your fear.

i braved the stupidest ocean. a man.
i waded in his stupid waters.

i took his stupid salt & let it
brine my skin, took his stupid

fish into my stupid hands & bit into it
like a stupid flapping plum. i kissed at

his stupid coral & stupid algae.
it was stupid. silly really. i knew nothing

that easy to get & good to feel
isn't also trying to eat you.

                        //

knew what could happen. needed
no snake. grew the fruit myself.

was the vine & the rain & the light.
the dirt was me. the hands drilling

into the dirt were my hands.
i made the blade that cut me down.

but i only knew how to live
when i knew how i'll die.

i want to live. think i mean it.
took the pill even on the days

i thought i wouldn't survive myself.
gave my body a shot. love myself

at least that much. thank you, me.
thank you, genvoya, my sea-foam savior.

thank you, sick blood, first husband, bff
dead river bright with salmon.

Patricia Smith
MAGA

I long for flay, shriek, the cottonwood drip. Tree sway. I
make my wants draw blood. Blanched yesterdays blare. They will—
great God, just wait 'til they do—take virtuous root, make
again my case for an unflinching America.
America, swerving so far past what God declared great,
will your mammies ever reek of cinnamon again,

will buck muscle ever split wide beneath lash again?
Again, I'm misunderstood. It's just that sometimes I
make too much of history's pious mandate, its great
eye for just the spurt of religion we require. Will
greatness, my *huge* greatness, deliver America?
America, is that even a question? Just make

Amer-ica that coiled pressure in a wronged throat, make
ideas squash your ideals, wind that clock backwards, again,
again, blur time to pallid rhythm. America,
will yourself sterile, tiki torch, thrust fist. Then when I
make red truth of lies, jogging your flawed recall, will
 "great again" mean "ours, not theirs," the sweet sight of ingrates

gratefully dimming to brown hush beneath our boots? "Great"
will slap those bellowing beasts to backdrop. I will make—
I swear—I'll make their black lives barely matter. I will.
America, let's be brash and unsullied again,
again let's swell the borders, smash the smaller, and I'll
make this sweet chaos whitefully ours. America,

make me your huge king. I'll give you back America,
America in straight lines, brash and ashen, its great
will to liberate thinner than its need to rule. I'm
greater than you dream—copper lord, master of remake.
I serve up the world you ache for, convince you again,
again, that rampant joy warrants the kill. So I will

again ask: *Hey, do you miss 1955?* Will
greatness unleashed finally release America?

America, go on, gaze into my gaze again,
make me dictum. You have to ignore our rumored great
will to be both foolish and fair. It has failed to make
"I" morph to "us." I have saved you. All there is is I.

I will make America great again.
America, I will make you great
again. Again, all there is is I.

Patricia Smith
Speak Now, Or Forever. Hold Your Peace.

*Two weeks after seventeen students were gunned down in Parkland, Florida,
hundreds of worshippers clutching AR-15's slurped holy wine and exchanged
or renewed wedding vows in a commitment ceremony at the World Peace and
Unification Sanctuary in Newfoundland, Pennsylvania.*

Draped in thick silk the hue of hemorrhage and bone, you fondle your butt
    stocks,
muffled lust needles your cheeks. Your aim? To make America great. Again,

your terse-lipped Lord has nudged you into the glare—numbed and witless in
    His name,
you preen and re-glue blessed unions, mistake America straight, contend

your unloosed crave for the sugared heat of triggers. Besotted beneath your
crowns of unspent shells, you hard-rhyme vows and quake, aware of that
    weight again,

the gawky, feral gush of fetish. Every uncocked groom and rigid bride
is greased and un-tongued, struck dumb by what's at stake. A miracle waits.
    You men

and women kaboom your hearts with skewered Spam and searing pink
    Walmart wine,
graze idly on ammo and blood-frosted cake. A prayer is the bait. *Amen*

woos guests in their ball gowns and bird suits, hallows your blind obsession
    with your
incendiary intended. Though you've faked America, hate upends

all this odd holy—its frayed altars, fumbled psalms, assault rifles chic in
itty veils. And we marvel at this outbreak, bewaring that gate again,

left unlatched so this bright foolish can flow through. This ilk of stupid blares
    blue
enough to rouse ancestors—y'all 'bout to make Amiri berate again,

'bout to conjure Fanny Lou and her tree-trunk wrists. While you snot-weep,
     caress
mute carbines, wed your unfathomable ache, America waits. 'Cause when

the sacrament cools, and the moon is pocked with giggling, who'll fall naked
     first,
whose shuddering tongue will dare the barrel? Take that dare. Consummate.
     And then,

whose blood will that be?

Patricia Smith
Saheed's Silver Gun

4/4/2018, Brooklyn: Police responded to a flurry of 911 calls that a man was randomly pointing a silver gun at people on the street. As they approached, the officers claimed that the man, thirty-four-year-old Saheed Vassell, "took a two-handed shooting stance and pointed" at them. In response, they fired ten rounds, killing Vassell, who was said to be struggling with mental health issues. It was then discovered that Vassell's "gun" was not a gun, but a bent pipe with an attached knob.

The heavy thing shimmered and shimmied in his hands,
clank sexy, like them kids say *unfuckwitable*, and Saheed

decided to play, see the skin shift on some folks, laugh
with them when the joke came clear. He crouched low,

sprang, pivoted, growled deep, folded his body behind
bodega doors, whipped his gorgeous gun up. He was

surely swayed by the prime-time weight of it, the barked
bangbang voice he gave the thing, and it was magic how

the havoc swelled, men dropping little leather bits of their
lives in the street as they backed away from him, Saheed,

and it wasn't his stink this time. It wasn't all those round
unknowable sounds that bundled like treasure in his throat

then hit the air with an overload of edge. Maybe he'd play
cowboy long enough to punch some breath from Brooklyn,

to spark a mannish giggle or two from the skirted women
who hiccup-screamed and locked onto his eyes like he held

not a fun gun, but a cocked black dick in his hands. Wait
'til he told them. Wait until they marveled at the day he

had managed to conjure, the squeals he had squeezed from
them with his bent shiny lie. He held it the way he'd seen

210

it held, like it could kill if it wanted, like one of them sassy
girls was waiting back in some hotel room for him to come

back strutting like semen and smoke, like a bad hombre just
hopped off the noon train searching for Saheed with the silver

star, like there was supposed to be stacks of drug cash in
the satchel, then *Hey, looks like it just ain't your day, buddy.*

Suddenly he was spooked by a scurry he didn't warrant, his
bad hombres all in hiding, huffing their tape-measured fear

from Starbucks and Duane Reade, glaring through plate
glass at just another beloved Crown Heights crazy and his

stupid silver gun, at its best a throwaway part of somebody's
toilet, and the good day exploded blue and beat at his eyes

to get in. By then he knew how long his name would live,
how it would die in the neck of anyone who loved it. He

felt the prissy storefronts prodding him forward. *I found
this thing*, he started to say, but by then all of him had

already spilled over the borders of his little drama. Now
all he was was blackblackblack gungungun and he wanted

to whisper *I found this thing*, but instead everyone heard
See what I did here? Sometimes my life wants out of this life.

Gary Soto
Campesino

Spring '17, I'm two time zones from my country
And hacking at the soldier-straight weeds—
I'm captain of their destruction. But the army
Of weeds keeps advancing, day after day.
I was a math teacher in Mexico,
But now I'm a number squeezed into a white van,
The stars blue as my life at 5:30 in the morning.
But don't feel sorry. I have my hands and back,
My face dark as a penny in a child's palm.
I walk in a straight row. My lean shadow keeps up.
But look at the circling seagulls,
Landlocked with no way home.

If there's work, I hoe nine hours in the beet fields,
Sometimes with a friend in the next row,
Sometimes alone. You would be crazy
To open your mouth—the wind and dust . . .
In a year, my face will be tooled like my wallet,
Dark and creased. Over the clods,
I sing to myself, or whistle like a parrot.
I practice English—
Waffle, no good tire, nice to meet you.

In the fields,
I stop when the patron on the tractor path says stop.
I pound sand from a boot like an hourglass.
Time pours forever and forever.
Tomorrow I'll start again. I'll chop at the earth
But it won't bleed under my hoe.
I'll chop, sweat and think in English.
Toaster, thread, seagulls find a way home.

Gary Soto
Christmas in East Los Angeles

In the front yard manger
Baby Jesus gripped a plastic rattle
And wore a Pampers a size too large.
The Christmas lights dangled like fruit
Over His glorious head.

The Three Kings hovered over the Prince of Peace.
The donkey smiled, the two lambs smiled.
The camel fallen on its side
Was smirking.

Mary and Joseph . . .
I looked up at the front window.
A woman worked a dishcloth over the glass,
Her own hair crowned with yellow light.
I made out a child running behind her.

On the trellis
Chili-shaped Christmas lights glowed.
The chicken in the yard blinked near the rose bush.
The family's Christmas soup?

I slid my hands into my pockets.
Someone was singing.
Someone was sweeping a porch.
Even I, a passerby, a sojourner,
A man who may end up in a diaper,
Breathed a halo into the morning air.
Peace comes to us all.

Mark Turcotte
It Burns

My mother did not like to be grabbed by her pussy. Or grabbed by her vagina, either. Not by that man, that last husband, so many years ago now, back on the reservation in that small log house, while bending over to poke the wood in her cook stove, or sun-pink arms raised to hang wash out on the line. I know this because she would jump and curse at him, slap at his hands, push him away when he giggled and tried to engulf her in his stupid or drunken arms. I know this because she would look for me to see whether I witnessed the assault, her disgrace. In mid-wrestle, her flimsy yellow house dress yanked above her waist, she whispered out to me with her glance something like, *I'm sorry my little boy*, or *please don't see*, or *grow up fast and crush this man with your knuckles*. It burned my eyes. So I learned to go blind to save her a sliver of the shame. I played by myself, drawing circles in the dirt with a stick, plotting, but it took me forever to grow my own deadly hands. I was too late.

The last time I saw my mother I read in a chair near her bedside or leaned close over her as she crossed back and forth between worlds. Tubed, tiny, twisted, her eyes wide to something beyond my shoulder. I straightened her flimsy yellow gown, held her cup to sip, eased my battered knuckles through her hair. After a time I asked her what she was looking at. I said, *Mother, please share it with me*. I listened to her lips move, say, *It burns, it burns, what I see*.

Mark Turcotte
Ezra Learns to Ride

In the same week that my lightning-eyed boy
firmly decides he is going to learn
how to ride his bicycle, my country
finally finds more people to blow
up and broadcast on TV.
So, as he shakes down the slope of our gravel
driveway, his feet bouncing off the pedals,
and crashes headfirst into a pot hole,
he does not curse or grumble like before, but stands up
fast, dusts himself off, maybe remembers the boy
we saw on the evening news still clutching his bicycle—
        broken boy at the bottom of a crater
        big as a bomb and dry as a well—
because he, my boy, he does not want to look
like that. He tries again.

Brian Turner
At Lowe's Home Improvement Center

Standing in aisle 16, the hammer and anchor aisle,
I bust a 50 pound box of double-headed nails
open by accident, their oily bright shanks
and diamond points like firing pins
from M-4s and M-16s.
                              In a steady stream
they pour onto the tile floor, constant as shells
falling south of Baghdad last night, where Bosch
kneeled under the chain guns of helicopters
stationed above, their tracer- fire a synaptic geometry
of light.
                    At dawn, when the shelling stops,
hundreds of bandages will not be enough.

                         . . .

Bosch walks down aisle 16 now, in full combat gear,
improbable, worn out from fatigue, a rifle
slung at his side, his left hand guiding
a ten-year-old boy who sees what war is
and will never clear it from his head.
Here, Bosch says, *Take care of him.*
I'm going back in for more.

                         . . .

Sheets of plywood drop with the airy breath
of mortars the moment they crack open
in shrapnel. Mower blades are just mower blades
and the Troy-Bilt Self-Propelled Mower doesn't resemble
a Black Hawk or an Apache. In fact, no one seems to notice
the casualty collection center Doc High marks out
in ceiling fans, aisle 15. Wounded Iraqis with IVs
sit propped against boxes as 92 sample Paradiso fans
hover in a slow revolution of blades.

The forklift driver over-adjusts, swinging the tines
until they slice open gallons and gallons of paint,
Sienna Dust and Lemon Sorbet and Ship's Harbor Blue
pooling in the aisle where Sgt. Rampley walks through—
carrying someone's blown-off arm cradled like an infant,
handing it to me, saying, *Hold this, Turner,*
we might find who it belongs to.

. . .

Cash registers open and slide shut
with a sound of machine guns being charged.
Dead soldiers are laid out at the registers,
on the black conveyor belts,
and people in line still reach
for their wallets. Should I stand
at the magazine rack, reading
Landscaping with Stone or *The Complete*
Home Improvement Repair Book?
What difference does it make if I choose
tumbled travertine tile, Botticino marble,
or Black Absolute granite. Outside,
palm trees line the asphalt boulevards,
restaurants cool their patrons who will enjoy
fireworks exploding over Bass Lake in July.

. . .

Aisle number 7 is a corridor of lights.
Each dead Iraqi walks amazed
by Tiffany posts and Bavarian pole lights.
Motion-activated incandescents switch on
as they pass by, reverent sentinels of light,
Fleur De Lis and Luminaire Mural Extérieur
welcoming them to Lowe's Home Improvement Center,
aisle number 7, where I stand in mute shock,
someone's arm cradled in my own.
                              The Iraqi boy beside me
reaches down to slide his fingertip in Retro Colonial Blue,
an interior latex, before writing
T, for *Tourniquet,* on my forehead.

Brian Turner
Ajal

—the appointed time of death which Muslims believe
God has determined for every individual; it cannot be
delayed or hastened.

There are ninety-nine special names for God,
my son, and not so long ago, I held you,
newly born, under the light of a crescent moon,
and gave you the name which means *servant*
of God, and I did not speak of war,
though tanks rolled in a mechanical thunder
of iron, and helicopters fired missiles
over the rooftops of our city—I whispered
the call to prayer in your right ear,
the summons to prayer in your left.

It should not be like this. Abd Allah,
many, many years from now, your own children
should wash your body three times
after your death. They should seal your mouth
with cotton, reciting prayers in a wash
of light and grieving, a perfume of lemons
and jasmine on your skin.

It should not be like this, Abd Allah.
I wanted you to see the Arch of Ctesiphon,
the tower of Samarra, the Ziggurat in Ur.
I wanted to teach you the history
of our family, to see where you might take it.
I wanted to show you the stars of Babylon,
to teach what was once taught to me.

I cannot undo what the shrapnel has done.
And so I climb down into this crumbling earth
to turn your face toward Mecca, as it must be,
and to whisper to you one last time, my son.
Remember the old words I have taught you,

Abd Allah. And go with your mother now,
who lies buried here beside you—
she will know the way.

Chase Twichell
The Ends of the World

When planes bound for Europe
take off late at night flying due west,

their sound comes to me
as wind in deep winter, slanting
the snow in the empty woods,

forming bright scars, ridges of drift.

Then I wake in the tropics'
air-conditioned chill.

When some grief overtakes me,
my mind flees north
to the clear-crashing brooks,

sun and shucked-off ice,
seeds splitting in the compost.

It was real. I lived there
when any moving water
was safe to drink.

Look, here come some jet skis,
gunning up to the public boat launch.

In this world, the mango sky
silhouettes the glass and steel
aspirations of our kind,

then weakens over the towers,
the derricks and cargo ships.

Just look at the guttering back of the bay,
and all that flees from it—

grand wound festering—what a sunset!

Even the mango's abandoning the sky,
hitching a final ride
on the clouds' undersides.

At first I raged at a single soda bottle
aloft on a see-through wave.

Now I no longer want to see
the illusion of the ocean intact,

the not-blue not-green water
breaking open and closing again,
restless above its heart of garbage,

the frothing white sucking edge

depositing a toothbrush, flip-flop,
bald head of a doll, and the usual
deflated jellyfish of condoms,

shoals of cigarette filters still intact
after who knows how long at sea,

a vast and senseless migration—
inedible, immortal, everywhere.

Part of me wants to see the city
gone entirely dark, glittering tableaux
extinguished, nothing but ruins,

colorless permanent shadows
inhabiting the empty streets.

How hard I fall out of sleep,
out of a vision of the earth restored.

I open my eyes in the dark, and find myself
back in the Garden of Earthly Delights,
naked again among stingers and fangs,

extinct and future creatures, all of us
unnamed and equal under the only sky.

But art can't resurrect it.
It only dreams it.

It hands a drunk an empty bottle.

Chase Twichell
The New Dark Ages

Thunderstorms stir me up—
the stillness right before

the first close tremor,
the pond shivering

at the height of summer,
the field full-blown, going to seed.

But this storm scares me.
A foreign climate occupies the land.

When nature was God, in my childhood,
I wasn't afraid. Snow buried the town,

the river flooded it,
lightning set the woods on fire.

In months the damage bandaged itself
with mosses and ferns, or got rebuilt.

This storm comes from another
world, here by mistake,

its rain blistering the birch leaves.
Has it been weaponized?

No one knows what to expect
of a storm with human parents.

Pamela Uschuk
A History of Morning Clouds and Contrails

So you think that you can live remote
from city streets paved with bullet casings,
the beheadings of girls sprayed from cable TV.

While the intricate lace burka of contrails smothers dawn's blush,
sky blasts dogma to smithereens over mountains
too distant to notice the woman barricaded
down the road at Fox Fire,
her automatic rifle aimed at police.

Each morning, ravens carve black questions
that go unanswered by light. Assailed
by head winds, they sheer, intent on laughter
as they bank nearly upside down to sing.

Sun climbs hand over burning hand
through aspen leaves going to gold bullion
anyone can spend regardless
of what bank they believe in.

Go out, lie in last season's sinking tomato bed, pull
dead plants around you and spit seeds
at the chemical ooze of contrails jets expel
bisecting the blue intelligence of sky's water dreams,
crosshatching quadrants between clouds
gauzy as love slipping between finger cracks.

The woman is desperate, mistakes bullets
she jams in her ex-husband's gun for
her own screams, for his incessant fists.   She, too,
inhales toxins saturating sky.

Lean to the warmth of an otter's last dive
before ice takes the river, the exhausted heart of the land.
Turn off all killing screens, what we've
relinquished in the name of security,
manipulating what we deep breathe.

Pamela Uschuk
Cracking 100

Near the border, preschoolers worry about butterflies.
How can they fly over the wall? Fifty feet tall, thick steel plates
would sear delicate wings. And, lizards, Miss,
how can they get through?
Small fingers draw orange wings crashing into steel,
lizards hanging their blue heads. *Y el tigre?*
Severing ancient migration paths, the wall
will ensure the jaguar's end.

Just after Cinco de Mayo, daytime temps
crack the knuckles of 100, ten degrees above normal.
No wall can stop rising heat, the death of coral reefs
or the governor calling for the National Guard to secure the border.
In holding cells, children separated from deported parents
wait for a future no one can predict.
And, in the San Joaquin Valley, strawberries and tomatoes
rot in fields. Farmers wonder where the pickers have gone.

Immaculate in his Armani suit, the President tweets
for Congressional support to build his wall, calls for
a prayer meeting in the Oval Office. You can hear
Bible hymns hum behind bulletproof doors
across the lush White House lawn where monarch butterflies,
who've migrated all the way from Mexico, land
on bright rose petals tended by hands
the same color as earth that nourishes them.

Elisabet Velasquez
Self-Portrait of America as a Revival

Mami never misses a revival.
It is a chance to pray
to dead things
like her marriage.
Her body,
a thing she carries like a cross.

In America
the police kill
men sometimes.
They do not
bring them back to life.
They still want to be called God.

I am a poet
obsessed with learning
a holy language.
A language that is not
white. I only speak in color.
      In Brooklyn.

        In resurrection.

I am a girl who cannot drown.
This makes them call me witch.
I make them call me baptized.
I come from hell
before the flame was gentrified.
I still remember when the block was hot.

The Bible teaches me to brag of riches
even if I am broke.
Even if I must die
to see it.
Which is to say—I own a piece of heaven

      on layaway.

In Brooklyn a revival is held
in the deadliest part of town.
Tonight heaven is a bank.
Tonight someone will cash out.
Tonight we only praise the living.

Tomorrow the news is our bible.
Tomorrow another god is dead.
Tomorrow a street corner lights a dozen candles.
Tomorrow a wall takes the shape of a face.
Tomorrow a T-shirt is turned memorial.
This is how we resurrect the dead.

Next week a mother joins a march to save her children.
She marches like a commandment.
She dares you to break her.
Her children will know no other god before her.
Her face heavy and wooden. An arc amidst a flood of bodies.

At revivals, we praise
the living.
At revivals, we dare you to find a tomb

      to house   our gods.

Richard Villar
Manifesto after the Storm

for Barrio Paraíso, Fajardo, y Puerto Rico

For those of you
who still wonder why we dance,
I have to tell you—
joy is a quinto in the dark;

by candle, by flashlight, by a cell phone, dead
except to illuminate the skirts of the dancer
who hasn't done this in years;
and Beto, the drummer who tries to follow her and stumbles,
palms stinging from the effort;
or the sweat beading across Beto's forehead
in sicá rhythm. Barrio Paraíso has brought light

to answer back, to greet fango and bare feet
pounding earth back to insistent life.
We've been doing this since Yukiyú was a baby
tossing his toys across el Yunque
to protest the coming wind.

This is nothing new.
Hurakán is another way to say temper tantrum,
and even the existence of the monster to the north
is permitted. An ocean rolls its mighty mouth
away from Africa, and the tumbao begins anew.
You must deal with practicalities, but never let
practicalities deal with you. A human heartbeat
is protest against the storm. Always has been.
When the Saviors reach us, finally,

after braving the waves and cutting through
on ships the size of imperial imagination,
and they offer us white sugar, canned sausage,
paper towels, and army rations
instead of the mangoes from our own fincas

we will speak instead to the turtle in our dreams,
who is painted on the walls of our ribcages,
and ask her to pull libertad from her shell.

Look again. She's real. She never owed us
anything but feet to conjure all the light we'll ever need,
rising over Fajardo, illuminating the dancer, the poet,
the island remaking itself.

Ocean Vuong
The Gift

a b c   a b c   a b c

She doesn't know what comes after.
So we begin again:

a b c   a b c   a b c

But I can see the fourth letter:
a strand of black hair—unraveled
from the alphabet
& written
on her cheek.

Even now the nail salon
will not leave her: isopropyl acetate,
ethyl acetate, chloride, sodium lauryl
sulfate & sweat fuming
through her pink
I ♥ NY T-shirt.

a b c   a b c   a—the pencil snaps.

The *b* bursting its belly
as dark dust blows
through a blue-lined sky.

Don't move, she says, as she picks
a wing bone of graphite
from the yellow carcass, slides it back
between my fingers.
Again. & again

I see it: the strand of hair lifting
from her face . . . how it fell
onto the page—& lived
with no sound. Like a word.
I still hear it.

George Wallace
I am sorry Diane di Prima

I am sorry Diane di Prima there was no
revolution, we cleaned things up just
about enough to carry on, we forgot
your necessary guns and Buddha,
the revolution of the body and heart
was no match for clean sheets and
prosperity, we brought down the man
and filled the lakes back up with rainbow
trout, we unpolluted the sky, closed the
factories and gentrified the Lower East Side,
hell I think it was a Rockefeller uncovered
the Saw Mill River (have you seen the Bronx
River Parkway sparkling in the autumn sun),
we filled our gas tanks and bank accounts and
ran off to Cancún, into the mouths of our children
we poured laughter fireworks poetry and college
degrees, we forgot about filling our bathtubs up
with your grandpa's Marxism and coal, the life-
preserving waters of Sacco & Vanzetti went
down the drain, escaped us—we put aside
your revolutionary letters and let our cup
runneth over with patriotism and football,
and craft beer, yeah we let the old sins
back in—success for the many, fuck-all for
the few—until the few became the many
again and now it's fuck-all for everyone
except the fat cats and their plastic wives in
golf carts, country clubs, and private towers,
and all the cleanup we've done's about to get
undone—reach for the sky, the privileged few
are on high protected by their trolls and goons
and the rest of us hanging around the streets to fool
and to fuel, it's ten P.M., 3 drunks crossing Church Street
pull on a young girl's hijab and shout Trump Trump
Trump—and the blood in the eyes of the people,
and the anger in their mouths, is for each other,

not for the oppressors—just the way they like it—
and where is the precious seed of your revolution
now, Diane di Prima, when we really need it.

Afaa Michael Weaver
Blackberry Wine

for Joe

In the early morning after the evening shift,
the work of tending the needs of machines, the unkind
masters with no hearts, the messiah's failed promise—

    bankrupt Jesus, hold my hand, bankrupt Jesus
    in this unholy land, I'm counting bottle tops and boxes
    for the bosses, Sweet Jesus, mechanic of my soul

We rode the two blocks to Fort Avenue and then the right
to Mary's, the bar looking over the tracks, the harbor
a black water churning music we couldn't hear, the brackish
slap of chemicals, the dumped sweat and blood of hungry eyes
from around the world looking for work, for the steady life

of paychecks, bankbooks to keep in dresser drawers, a life
better than what the negroes were making, black folk
looking up from being beat down, taking what work is, a hard
way of paying the bills for what the soul needs, the love
to line up inside it, a glorious wallpaper, the spirit's silk skin—

    bankrupt Jesus, hold my hand, bankrupt Jesus
    in this unholy land, I'm counting bottle tops and boxes
    for the bosses, Sweet Jesus, mechanic of my soul

Mary opened the door to where we could sit with the whites,
an alpha omega carousel at the bar, or we could buy our own
and drive up past where the slave ships docked, past the blocks
still remembering naked feet washed down for selling south,
gone south they would say, sold, or just plain gone, stone gone

Mary with her silver hair in the bar now gone, the shipyards
gone, the rough way the white children called us *niggers* gone,
the clap of tow motors crossing the metal plates into the trucks,
fists going upside the heads of friends in corners we closed off
so the bosses wouldn't see us settling things like hard men—

bankrupt Jesus, hold my hand, bankrupt Jesus
in this unholy land, I'm counting bottle tops and boxes
for the bosses, Sweet Jesus, mechanic of my soul

Gone, crossed over the bridge into East Baltimore,
to an after-hours hand passing brown bags of liquor
and beer to us when Mary's was closed, gone home
to where the colors of skin in the day or night we knew
so much we could read each other, our lives like braille,

the alphabet of struggle etched in behind God's ears
when he missed a beat and we have to make up the sound
of what language is in the silence where hope abandons us,
where we abandon and cast out the sweet ones among us,
gay men who loved men in the hard pregnancy of labor—

bankrupt Jesus, hold my hand, bankrupt Jesus
in this unholy land, I'm counting bottle tops and boxes
for the bosses, Sweet Jesus, mechanic of my soul

Afaa Michael Weaver
Prayer for the City

The old bridge to Gino Marchetti's now
the ledge of a cliff, the mountain invisible

where I am ten years old, running as one
in a pack, holding cheap five & dime toys,

bottles breaking behind us, glass spreading
in the eyes of angels who would block death

if death were to appear, old man in a coat
from the London Fog outlet on Falls Road,

a harbinger in a sharkskin suit, and we run
as fast as boys can run, past me standing

here fifty years later, time an Oldsmobile 98,
a Buick Electra 225, time an Easter Parade,

our sisters with plaits and patent leather,
Vaseline on their legs, we in seersucker suits,

time a rolled-down window on Highway One
going south to a black Bethlehem where Jesus

is born every day in peanut fields like heads
of the unborn under the sun, unborn tongues

that will grow and sing the amazing grace songs
to charm death away from us. I see past the cliff

to alleys pristine with new cement to cover
the white flight to newer borders, white flight

from our black beauty, and over the trills,
the lilting sounds of children playing at war

there is history, a woman preacher
in a golden robe unfurling the books

of our lives, the undone righteousness
that sits on the stoops with us, waiting

for the frozen custard man in this world
our fathers and mothers made from the grist

of their fathers and mothers with flesh
parceled out from landing here in chains,

bound over to move mountains of faith
and make them the fountains of a love

children of masters do not know, children
chasing us back to the killing space

of what was once holy and now is most
high, above saintliness in a place where

there are no heavens and no easy outs
like hell. It is here we must live, sing.

Bruce Weigl
What Saves Us

We are wrapped around each other in
the back of my father's car parked
in the empty lot of the high school
of our failures, the sweat on her neck
like oil. The next morning I would leave
for the war and I thought I had something
coming for that, I thought to myself
that I would not die never having
been inside her long body. I pulled
her skirt above her waist like an umbrella
blown inside out by the storm. I pulled
her cotton panties up as high as
she could stand. I was on fire. Heaven
was in sight. We were drowning on our
tongues and I tried to tear my pants off
when she stopped so suddenly
we were surrounded only by my shuddering
and by the school bells grinding in the
empty halls. She reached to find something,
a silver crucifix on a silver
chain, the tiny savior's head hanging
and stakes through his hands and his feet.
She put it around my neck and held
me so long the black wings of my heart
were calmed. We are not always right
about what we think will save us.
I thought that dragging the angel down would
save me, but instead I carried the crucifix
in my pocket and rubbed it on my
face and lips nights the rockets roared in.

People die sometimes so near you
you feel them struggling to cross over,
the deep untangling, of one body from another.

Bruce Weigl
War Story

I'm waiting for the war to end for me. I'm waiting for the sound of rockets and mortars to stop rushing through my sleepless nights, for the crack of ambush to quiet, for the movement through the hazy trees to stop and then be nothing but sun coming up through waves of green and yellow bamboo by the river someone had fought hard to defend a thousand years before. I'm waiting for the dead

to stop turning from their places in harm's way, so I don't have to care for them anymore. I'm waiting for the war to end for me, the dreams of gun fire out of nowhere, the rounds that I feel in my back going in, the faces of the enemy so near, I can see the oil on their skin.

Someone give me something to take or tell me something to believe or teach me something to help forget, but we all know the truth about that now. How there is no way back from the knowing something right down to your soul, how there is no remedy for how the brain is twisted into a loop that will never end, at least this is what they tell us now.

Bruce Weigl
Wade Park VA

Rain slices through me as if I was the grassy field. No matter how many times you turn the key, the lock will not open. The birth of someone's hair piled high this morning on her head which she did with her only remaining arm and hand, VA hospital, Wade Park;

she's here in mental health with the rest of us, as if there were answers. There are no answers. She could have had help tying up her hair that way, on top of her head; I don't think you can do that with only one hand, but I may be wrong. People under duress do amazing things to save themselves from oblivion. Back outside

in the rain, nothing has changed. The woman who lost her arm to another war would not look up from the floor where she kept her eyes until the nurse called her name. She was tall when she stood up and her hair was wildly trying to free itself from the bun she had tied it into so carefully in the morning. Another turn of the wheel is all, and when it comes to rest this time, someone's arm is missing, and someone else's mind.

Eleanor Wilner
In a Time of War

Flies, caught in the sap of the living
tree, some day will be
precious, dressed in amber—just so
the past appears to the present, gem-
like in its perfect preservation,
the hardened gold of yesterday, a relic
through which today's sun shines.

But those who are caught in the sticky
sap of actual time, insects in the odds
against them, who struggle in the ooze,
slowly sink into the mass,
the numberless, anonymous dead . . .
till the atrocious becomes
the mundane, our senses numb
from the sheer litany of repetition . . .

let us, then, just watch this one small
desperate fly, stuck first by the feet,
and then, in its struggles, entangled
entirely in the glob of sap, its wings
heavy as a brass angel's, until it is
all at once still, a dark speck
in a bubble of sap
oozing from the felled tree
in a forest marked for the mill.

How many millennia will pass
before a teardrop lavaliere of amber
carrying its cargo of loss
will adorn the vanity of another
creature, the fly a fossil of a species
no longer present on the Earth,
the Earth itself a speck in a cosmos where
galaxies are carded like cotton on a comb
and pulled out into a distance

where some new fabric is being spun
and shimmers in the firelight
of countless, burning suns.

Eleanor Wilner
Establishment

Death had established himself in the Red Room,
the White House having become his natural
abode: chalk-white façade, pillars like the bones
of extinct empires, armed men crawling its halls
or looking down, with suspicion, from its roof;
its immense luxury, thick carpets, its plush velvet chairs—
all this made Death comfortable, bony as he is, a fact
you'd barely notice, his camouflage a veil of flesh
drawn over him, his tailor so adroit, and he so elegant,
so *GQ*, almost a dandy, so suited for the tables
where the crystal, silverware, the swans of ice gleamed
with the polished purity of light on precious things;
Death was the guest of honor here, confiding, convivial
among friends who leaned to light his cigar—his power
seemed their own, body counts at their command;
a power beyond even their boy-wet dreams
was now a custom they feared to lose: each saw
the world the way a hooded falcon on the fist
sees it, blind, waiting for the next release; one word
could bury villages alive, could send
battalions to an early grave—
                                                    so Death can rest
assured, smiling at such a harvest—and so
deliciously unseasonable, like berries in winter.
Welcome houseguest, he stretches his ancient
frame, warm under expensive wool, sipping wine,
picking his teeth with a last bone,
meat all the sweeter for being
the lambs of honor, corn-fed and unsuspecting;
or the children playing in the rubble
who reach down for a souvenir of steel
that has fallen from the sky—really,
Death has seldom had a better season or such
a winning score; he must see to their protection,
these little men who think to be *his* master—
flatter a fool and make him useful, he thinks,
and smiles benignly, whitely, at his hosts,

assuring them of his gratitude, his presence
at their councils, his everlasting support . . .
until, no longer able to hide
his triumph, his delight, forgetting the flesh
he has clothed himself in for the occasion,
he rubs his hands together
in the ancient gesture of satisfaction,
naked bone on bone—how the sound grates,
how the grateful sparks fly!

Eleanor Wilner
This Straw and Manure World

And the mare kicks at her traces, pulling the old-fashioned rig
      around Independence Hall, surrounded now by cheap aluminum
stands, fences to hold off terrorists, another fool's errand on which
      Smokey the Bear and his brethren, with their self-important official hats,
have been sent: the terrorists don't give a damn about our little historic
      pile of bricks and sentiment, from a time before empire, when
18th century men, in what was hopefully called The Enlightenment, made
      their stand for autonomy, more economic than ideal, but sanctified by time
and by an empire's need for roots with some morality clinging to them—
      not just dirt. There was a prediction, back in Franklin's time, that if
the population grew at the current rate, the amount of horse manure
      would be, in another century, 18 feet deep. They weren't entirely wrong.
Though they didn't factor in the steam engine, Henry Ford, or the trolley car,
      they guessed right on the depth of horseshit, though most of it is in D.C.,
our new, Imperial capital: where the Washington Monument, white towering
      obelisk, glowers with its red electric eyes, a Klansman in a white hood,
staring down the blossoming Mall, admiring its reflection
      in the monumental pool.

Daisy Zamora
Death Abroad

for Francisco Zamora Gámez
and Rogelio Ramírez Mercado

What lit landscapes, what waters, what lush greens,
what kite flying loose against the sun
in a blue morning journey?

What furious storm, what distant summer
dazzling with waves and salt air,
what dark tree-lined streets, what cool intimacy
of a garden, what evenings?

Which moon among moons,
which night of definitive love
under the splendor of stars?

What voices, what murmuring laughter and footsteps,
what faces grown distant, what familiar streets,
what blissful daybreak in a half-lit room,
what books, what songs?

What final nostalgia,
what last vision illuminated your sight
when death lowered your eyelids
in that strange land?

—translated by George Evans

Daisy Zamora
Salvadoran Woman Killed on Fillmore Street

She ran as fast as she could, she
shouted into the void, *Oh God—*
she worked so hard that day—
tightly held her purse against
her breast, then fell
in a pool of blood.

Afterwards, the kids told the police:
We didn't want to stab her we were just
desperate we only wanted her money
but she screamed so hard
she scared the hell out, she really
scared the hell out of us.

Her children were devastated, their
only support she worked double shifts
that day had forty bucks in her purse
they were waiting for her on the way
to the grocery store it was New Year's Eve,
end of the millennium.

The newspaper also published the menu
of the dinner
       the mayor of San Francisco
       was giving that night.

Of the many delicacies listed
       was
       wild salmon fillets
       sprinkled with genuine gold
            dust.

Acknowledgments

All possible care has been taken to trace ownership and secure permission for the poems reproduced in this book. Many of these poems are published here for the first time. The author and publisher would like to thank the following organizations and individuals for permission to reprint the following copyrighted material. (This page constitutes a continuation of the copyright page.)

Elizabeth Alexander, "Smile." First published in *Crave Radiance* (Graywolf Press, 2010). Copyright © 2010, 2019 by Elizabeth Alexander. Reprinted with the permission of the author.

Julia Alvarez, "Refugee Women," from *WITNESS*, special issue, "Exile in America" (2006). Copyright © 2006 by Julia Alvarez. Reprinted by permission of Susan Bergholz Literary Services, New York, N.Y., and Lamy, N.M. All rights reserved.

Doug Anderson, "Binge," "How Nazis," and "Subterranean Inner Redneck Blues." Copyright © 2019 by Doug Anderson. Reprinted with the permission of the author.

Naomi Ayala, "Vending" and "They Roll the Tarp." Copyright © 2019 by Naomi Ayala. Reprinted with the permission of the author.

Benjamin Balthaser, "Ghazal for Jim Foley #5: What Comes Home." Copyright © 2019 by Benjamin Balthaser. Reprinted with the permission of the author.

Sean Bates, "The Face I Wore." Copyright © 2019 by Sean Bates. Reprinted with the permission of the author.

Jan Beatty, "Trumpcare" (previously uncollected), copyright © 2019 by Jan Beatty. "I Knew I Wasn't Poor" from *Jackknife: New and Selected Poems* (University of Pittsburgh Press, 2017); copyright © 2017 by Jan Beatty. Reprinted with the permission of the author.

Tara Betts, "Failed Spells." Copyright © 2019 by Tara Betts. Reprinted with the permission of the author.

Richard Blanco, "Dreaming a Wall," originally published in *Boundaries* by Richard Blanco (Two Ponds Press), and "Complaint of El Río Grande," originally published in *How to Love a Country* by Richard Blanco (Beacon Press). Copyright © 2019 by Richard Blanco. Reprinted with the permission of the author.

Rafael Campo, "II. Jamal," "IV. Kelly," "VII. Manuel," and "XI. Jane Doe #2" from "Ten Patients and Another," "The Chart," and "The Good Doctor." Copyright © 2019 by Rafael Campo. Reprinted with the permission of the author.

Cyrus Cassells, "The World That the Shooter Left Us." Copyright © 2019 by Cyrus Cassells. Reprinted with the permission of the author.

Contributors

Elizabeth Alexander—poet, educator, memoirist, scholar, and cultural advocate—is president of the Andrew W. Mellon Foundation. She has held distinguished professorships at Smith College, Columbia University, and Yale University, where she taught for fifteen years and chaired the African American Studies Department. She is a Chancellor of the Academy of American Poets, serves on the Pulitzer Prize Board, and co-designed the Art for Justice Fund. Notably, Alexander composed and delivered "Praise Song for the Day" for the inauguration of President Barack Obama in 2009, and is the author or coauthor of fourteen books. Her book of poems, *American Sublime*, was a finalist for the Pulitzer Prize for Poetry in 2006, and her memoir, *The Light of the World*, was a finalist for the Pulitzer Prize for Biography in 2015.

Julia Alvarez writes about childhood memories and the experience of being an immigrant living between two cultures, those of the Dominican Republic and the United States. She has also written a number of novels, including *How the García Girls Lost Their Accents* and *In the Time of the Butterflies*, which was adapted into a motion picture.

Doug Anderson won the Kate Tufts Discovery Award for *The Moon Reflected Fire* and a grant from the Academy of American Poets for *Blues for Unemployed Secret Police*. Most recently, he is the author of the memoir *Keep Your Head Down: Vietnam, the Sixties, and a Journey of Self-Discovery* and of the poetry collection *Horse Medicine*.

Naomi Ayala is the recipient of numerous awards and fellowships and the author of three books of poetry: *Wild Animals on the Moon*, *This Side of Early*, and *Calling Home: Praise Songs and Incantations*. She works with innovative youth programs and makes her living as an education consultant, translator, and teacher.

Benjamin Balthaser is an associate professor of multiethnic literature at Indiana University, South Bend. He is the author of *Anti-Imperialist Modernism: Race and Transnational Radical Culture from the Great Depression to the Cold War* and of a collection of poems titled *Dedication*. His critical and creative work has appeared in journals or magazines including *Boston Review*, *Massachusetts Review*, *Minnesota Review*, *Criticism*, *Jacobin*, and *American Quarterly*.

Sean Bates grew up in various restaurants across upstate New York. His forthcoming collection considers the inherited idea of work, as well as the inherited debt. He received his M.F.A. from the University of Massachusetts Amherst and completed his undergraduate studies at Oberlin College. He currently resides in Florence, Massachusetts, with his wife, Elizabeth, and their cat Smudge.

Jan Beatty's fifth book, *Jackknife: New and Collected Poems*, won the 2018 Paterson Prize. *The Switching/Yard* was named by *Library Journal* one of *30 New Books That Will Help You Rediscover Poetry*. The *Huffington Post* named her one of ten women writers for "required reading." Books include *Red Sugar*, *Boneshaker*, and *Mad River*. Beatty has worked as a waitress, a welfare caseworker, and a social worker and teacher in maximum-security prisons.

Tara Betts is the author of *Break the Habit, Arc & Hue*, and *Refuse to Disappear*. She is a coeditor of *The Beiging of America: Personal Narratives about Being Mixed Race in the Twenty-First Century* and editor of Philippa Duke Schuyler's long-out-of-print memoir *Adventures in Black and White*. She has taught at Rutgers University, University of Illinois–Chicago, Chicago State University's M.F.A. Program, and with the Prison + Neighborhood Arts Program at Stateville Prison.

Richard Blanco, selected by President Obama as the fifth inaugural poet in U.S. history, is the youngest and the first Latino, immigrant, and gay person to serve in such a role. He was born in Madrid to Cuban exile parents and raised in Miami, and the negotiation of cultural identity and nationhood characterizes Blanco's numerous prized collections of poetry and memoirs. The poems appearing in this anthology are from his latest book, *How to Love a Country*.

Rafael Campo teaches and practices general internal medicine at Harvard Medical School, where he also directs the literature and writing programs in the Arts and Humanities Initiative, and at Beth Israel Deaconess Medical Center in Boston. Campo is the author of *What the Body Told, Diva, The Enemy*, and *Alternative Medicine*. He is the recipient of a Guggenheim Fellowship, a Pushcart Prize, the Paterson Poetry Prize, and two Lambda Literary Awards. His new and selected volume of poems is *Comfort Measures Only*.

Cyrus Cassells is the author of six books: *The Mud Actor, Soul Make a Path through Shouting, Beautiful Signor, More Than Peace and Cypresses, The Crossed-Out Swastika*, and *The Gospel according to Wild Indigo*. His book of Catalan translations, *Still Life with Children: Selected Poems of Francesc Parcerisas*, was published in March 2019. He is the recipient of a Lannan Literary Award, a William Carlos Williams Award, and a Lambda Literary Award.

Hayan Charara is the author of three poetry books, most recently *Something Sinister*, and editor of *Inclined to Speak*, an anthology of contemporary Arab American poetry. He is a series editor and cofounder, with Fady Joudah, of the Etel Adnan Poetry Prize. Born in Detroit, he lived for many years in New York City and now makes his home in Houston.

Chen Chen's work has appeared in two chapbooks and in such publications as *Poetry, Gulf Coast, Indiana Review, Best of the Net*, and *The Best American Poetry*. The recipient of the 2016 A. Poulin Jr. Poetry Prize, he has also been awarded fellowships from Kundiman, the Saltonstall Foundation, and Lambda Literary; he was a finalist for the Ruth Lilly and Dorothy Sargent Rosenberg Poetry Fellowships in 2015. His most recent poetry collection, *When I Grow Up I Want to be a List of Further Possibilities*, was longlisted for the National Book Award for Poetry.

Brian Clements is the author, most recently, of *A Book of Common Rituals*, and one of the editors of *Bullets into Bells: Poets and Citizens Respond to Gun Violence*. He is Professor of Writing, Linguistics, and Creative Process at Western Connecticut State University, where he founded and coordinated the M.F.A. in Creative and Professional Writing. He lives in Connecticut, where his wife, Abbey (a teacher), survived the Sandy Hook shooting.

Jim Daniels's recent poetry books include *Rowing Inland, Street Calligraphy*, and *The Middle Ages*. He is the author of six collections of fiction and four produced screenplays, and the editor of several anthologies, including *Challenges to the Dream*, which publishes the best of the Martin Luther King Jr. Day Writing Awards, a competition for high school and college students that he founded in 1999.

Kwame Dawes is the author of twenty-one collections of poetry and numerous books of fiction, criticism, and essays. A professor of English at the University of Nebraska, he is Glenna Luschei Editor of *Prairie Schooner*, a series editor of the African Poetry Book Series, and artistic director of the Calabash International Literary Festival. His most recent collection, *City of Bones: A Testament* (Northwestern University Press), appeared in 2017. In 2018 Dawes was elected a Chancellor for the Academy of American Poets and named a Fellow of the Royal Society of Literature. In 2019 Dawes won the Windham-Campbell Prize for poetry.

Chard deNiord is the author of the poetry collections *The Double Truth, Night Mowing, Sharp Golden Thorn, Asleep in the Fire*, and *Interstate*. His poetry has appeared in *The Pushcart Prize, The Best Poems from Thirty Years of the Pushcart Prize, The Best American Poetry*, and in numerous journals. He is a professor of English and creative writing at Providence College and cofounder of the New England College M.F.A. program in poetry.

Dante Di Stefano is the author of the poetry collections *Love Is a Stone Endlessly in Flight* and *Ill Angels*. Along with María Isabel Álvarez, he edited the anthology *Misrepresented People: Poetic Responses to Trump's America*.

Kathy Engel is a poet and cultural worker whose books include *Ruth's Skirts; We Begin Here: Poems for Palestine and Lebanon*, which she edited with Kamal Boullata; *The Kitchen*, with art by German Pérez; and a chapbook, *Banish the Tentative*. *The Lost Brother Alphabet* will appear in March 2020. She teaches in the Department of Art and Public Policy, Tisch School of the Arts, NYU.

George Evans has published poetry collections, including *The New World* and *Sudden Dreams*, in the United States and England. *Espejo de la tierra / Earth's Mirror*, a bilingual selection, was published in Costa Rica. He translated *The Violent Foam*, by his wife, Nicaraguan poet Daisy Zamora; co-translated *The Time Tree*, by Vietnamese poet Huu Thinh; and was editor and director of the national public arts project *Streetfare Journal*. His writing awards include grants and fellowships from the National Endowment for the Arts, the California Arts Council, the Lannan Foundation, and a Japanese government *Monbusho* Fellowship.

Tarfia Faizullah is the author of the poetry collections *Seam* and *Registers of Illuminated Villages*. She was born in Brooklyn to Bangladeshi immigrants and raised in Texas. Her writing appears widely and has been translated into multiple languages and displayed at the Smithsonian, the Rubin Museum of Art, and elsewhere.

Carolyn Forché is an American poet, editor, translator, and activist. Her books of poetry are *Blue Hour*, *The Angel of History*, *The Country between Us*, and *Gathering the Tribes*. In 2013, Forché received the Academy of American Poets Fellowship, and in 2017, she became one of the first two poets to receive the Windham-Campbell Prize. She is a professor at Georgetown University and lives in Maryland with her husband, the photographer Harry Mattison.

Denice Frohman is a poet and performer from New York City. She is a CantoMundo Fellow and former Women of the World Poetry Slam Champion. Her poems have appeared in *Nepantla: An Anthology for Queer Poets of Color*, *Women of Resistance: Poems for a New Feminism*, *The Adroit Journal*, and elsewhere. Frohman has been featured on hundreds of stages from the White House to the Apollo, and is one of the organizers of #PoetsforPuertoRico.

Danielle Legros Georges is a poet, educator, and translator. Appointed Boston's second Poet Laureate in 2015, she is a professor of creative writing and the director of Lesley University's M.F.A. program in creative writing. Her work includes collaborations with literary and visual artists, museums, and galleries. Her honors include fellowships from the Massachusetts Cultural Council, the Boston Foundation, the Black Metropolis Research Consortium, and commissions from the Trustees of Reservations and the Boston Public Library. She is the author of two books of poems, *The Dear Remote Nearness of You* and *Maroon* and the chapbook *Letters from Congo*; she is the editor of *City of Notions: An Anthology of Contemporary Boston Poems*.

Maria Mazziotti Gillan, American Book Award recipient for *All That Lies Between Us*, is the author of twenty-three books. She founded the Poetry Center in Paterson, New Jersey, and is the editor of the *Paterson Literary Review*. Gillan was appointed a Bartle Professor and professor emerita of English and creative writing at Binghamton University–SUNY; her recent publications include *What Blooms in Winter* and a poetry and photography collaboration with Mark Hillringhouse, *Paterson Light and Shadow*.

Aracelis Girmay is the author of three books of poems: *Teeth*, *Kingdom Animalia*, and *the black maria*. She is on the editorial board of the African Poetry Book Fund. She teaches and lives with her family in New York.

Ruth Goring is the author of the poetry collections *Soap Is Political* and *Yellow Doors*; her poems have appeared in *RHINO*, *Calyx*, *Iron Horse Literary Review*, and many other publications. She is the author of a children's picture book, *Adriana's Angels / Los ángeles de Adriana*, and author/illustrator of another, *Picturing God*. Goring is involved in a Chicago neighborhood group organizing against ICE incursions, and in human rights causes in Colombia, where she grew up.

Adam Grabowski's work has appeared in *jubilat*, *DMQ Review*, *The Rattling Wall*, and elsewhere. His poem "Individualized Education Program" is featured in the anthology *Alongside We Travel: Contemporary Poets on Autism*, edited by Sean Thomas Dougherty. Adam teaches poetry at the Pioneer Valley Writers' Workshop and is currently a candidate for an M.F.A. in writing at the Vermont College of Fine Arts. He lives with his wife and daughters in Holyoke, Massachusetts.

torrin a. greathouse is a transgender cripple-punk poet and M.F.A. candidate at the University of Minnesota. She is the author of *boy/girl/ghost* (TAR Chapbook Series, 2018) and winner of the Peseroff Poetry Prize, Palette Poetry Prize, and the Naugatuck River Narrative Poetry Prize. Their work has or will appear in *POETRY*, the *New York Times*, *Poem-a-Day*, *Foglifter*, and the *Kenyon Review*.

Laurie Ann Guerrero is the author of *Tongue in the Mouth of the Dying* and *A Crown for Gumecindo*. She served consecutively as the Poet Laureate of San Antonio, from 2014 to 2016, and then of the State of Texas from 2016 to 2017. Guerrero holds an M.F.A. in poetry from Drew University and is the writer-in-residence at Texas A&M University–San Antonio.

Donald Hall (1928–2018) served as Poet Laureate of New Hampshire from 1984 to 1989 and as Poet Laureate of the United States from 2006 to 2007. He was the author of numerous collections of poetry, essays, fiction, plays, and children's books. He was also a noted baseball writer. His poetry collection *Without* chronicles the early death of his wife, the poet Jane Kenyon. Winner of two Guggenheim fellowships, the Los Angeles Times Book Prize for poetry, the National Book Critics Circle Award, the Robert Frost Medal, and the Ruth Lilly Poetry Prize, Hall lived and worked at Eagle Pond Farm, his ancestral home in New Hampshire.

Sam Hamill (1943–2018), the founding editor of Copper Canyon Press, published more than forty books, including seventeen volumes of poetry, literary essays, and translations from classical Chinese, Japanese, Greek, Latin, Estonian, and Vietnamese. In 2003, declining an invitation to the White House, he founded Poets Against the War, collecting 30,000 poems by 26,000 poets, the largest anthology in recorded history. A book of his collected poems, *Habitation*, was published by Lost Horse Press in 2014. He lived in Anacortes, Washington.

Samuel Hazo is a poet, editor, translator, critic, playwright, and essayist as well as the founder of the International Poetry Forum in Pittsburgh. He taught English at Duquesne University for forty-three years. Born in 1928, he began writing poetry during the Korean War. His poetry collection *Once for the Last Bandit* was a National Book Award finalist. He is also known for *The Song of the Horse: Selected Poems 1958–2008* and as the translator of Adonis and Nada Tueni.

Marcelo Hernandez Castillo is the author of *Cenzontle*, winner of numerous prizes, including the Golden Poppy award from the NCIBA, and of the Drinking Gourd Chapbook Poetry Prize winner *Dulce* (Northwestern, 2018). His memoir *Children of the Land* is forthcoming. As one of the founders of the Undocupoets campaign, he received the Barnes and Noble "Writers for Writers" Award and was the first undocumented student to graduate from the Helen Zell Writers Program at the University of Michigan. He lives in Marysville, California, where he teaches poetry.

Juan Felipe Herrera, son of migrant farmworkers Felipe Emilio Herrera and María de la Luz Quintana, was the California Poet Laureate from 2012 to 2015 and Poet Laureate of the United States thereafter, from 2015 to 2017. His book *Every Day We Get More Illegal* is forthcoming from City Lights.

Jane Hirshfield's eighth poetry book, *The Beauty*, was long-listed for the 2015 National Book Award. Her honors include fellowships from the Guggenheim and Rockefeller Foundations, the NEA, and the Academy of American Poets, as well as nine selections in *The Best American Poetry*. A chancellor emerita of the Academy of American Poets, Hirshfield founded #PoetsForScience in spring 2017. Her work appears in the *New Yorker*, *The Atlantic*, the *New Republic*, *Poetry*, the *Times Literary Supplement*, and elsewhere.

Everett Hoagland has written *Black Velvet, This City and Other Poems*, and more recently *Here: New and Selected Poems* and *Ocean Voices: An Anthology of Ocean Poems*. A professor of English at the University of Massachusetts–Dartmouth for more than thirty years, he served as the inaugural Poet Laureate of New Bedford. His awards include the Gwendolyn Brooks Award, the Distinguished Service to University Award from UMass Dartmouth, and the Langston Hughes Society Award.

Lawrence Joseph was born in Detroit of Lebanese and Syrian heritage. He is the author of six books of poetry, most recently *So Where Are We?*, and two books of prose—*Lawyerland*, a nonfiction novel, and *The Game Changed: Essays and Other Prose*, in the University of Michigan Press's Poets on Poetry Series. *A Certain Clarity: Selected Poems* is forthcoming. He is Tinnelly Professor of Law at St. John's University School of Law, where he teaches labor and employment law. He lives in New York City.

Yusef Komunyakaa is the author of numerous books of poetry, including *Taboo, Dien Cai Dau, Neon Vernacular* (for which he received the Pulitzer Prize), *Warhorses, The Chameleon Couch, Testimony*, and most recently, *The Emperor of Water Clocks*. His honors include the William Faulkner Prize (Université Rennes, France), the Ruth Lilly Poetry Prize, and the Wallace Stevens Award. His plays, performance art, and libretti have been performed internationally and include *Saturnalia, Testimony*, and *Gilgamesh*. He teaches at New York University.

Dorianne Laux is the author of *The Book of Men*, winner of the Paterson Poetry Prize, *Facts about the Moon*, winner of the Oregon Book Award, *Awake, What We Carry*, and *Smoke*. Her most recent anthology is *Only as the Day Is Long: New and Selected Poems*. She teaches poetry in the M.F.A. Program at North Carolina State University and is part of the founding faculty at Pacific University's Low Residency M.F.A. Program.

Adrian C. Louis (1946–2018), an enrolled member of the Lovelock Paiute Tribe, was born and raised in northern Nevada. Originally a journalist and poet, he was a professor of English at the Minnesota State University in Marshall from 1999 to his retirement in 2014. He wrote twelve books of poems and two works of fiction: *Wild Indians and Other Creatures*, short stories; and *Skins*, a novel later turned into a feature film.

Ricardo Alberto Maldonado was born and raised in Puerto Rico. He is the translator of Dinapiera Di Donato's *Colaterales / Collateral*, the author of *The Life Assignment*, and the recipient of poetry fellowships from Queer/Arts/Mentorship and the New York Foundation for the Arts.

Paul Mariani is the author of more than 250 essays, introductions, and reviews, as well as scholarly chapters in anthologies and encyclopedias; biographies of William Carlos Williams, John Berryman, Robert Lowell, Hart Crane, Gerard Manley Hopkins, and Wallace Stevens; seven volumes of poetry, most recently *Epitaphs for the Journey*; and a spiritual memoir, *Thirty Days: On Retreat with the Exercises of St. Ignatius*. His awards include fellowships from the Guggenheim Foundation and the NEA and NEH, and the John Ciardi Award for Lifetime Achievement in Poetry. His most recent book is *The Mystery of It All: The Vocation of Poetry in the Twilight of Modernity*.

Demetria Martínez is a New Mexico–based author and activist who has published two books of poetry, *Breathing between the Lines* and *The Devil's Workshop*, and coauthored an award-winning bilingual children's book with Rosalee Montoya. Her novel *Mother Tongue* is based in part upon her experiences as a reporter covering the Sanctuary Movement—activism by citizens who defied immigration law by aiding refugees fleeing Central America—and the subsequent trial in which she was accused of smuggling Salvadoran refugees into the country. A jury acquitted her on First Amendment grounds.

Paul Martínez Pompa earned an M.F.A. in creative writing at Indiana University, where he served as a poetry editor for the *Indiana Review* and was awarded a Dean's Minority Fellowship. His publications include the chapbook *Pepper Spray* and a full-length debut, *My Kill Adore Him*, winner of the 2008 Andres Montoya Poetry Prize. He lives in Chicago and teaches composition, poetry, and creative writing at Triton College in River Grove, Illinois.

Julio Marzán has published two poetry books, *Translations without Originals* and *Puerta de Tierra*, and has been widely anthologized. From 2004 to 2007 he was Poet Laureate of Queens, N.Y. Under the pen name J.A. Marzán, he has published *The Bonjour Gene*, a novel in stories, and the satirical "Newyorican" novel *Don't Let Me Die in Disneyland: The 3-D Life of Eddie Loperena*, in which first appeared the poem "Don't Let Me Die in Disneyland."

Marty McConnell is the author of *Gathering Voices: Creating a Community-Based Poetry Workshop* and *when they say you can't go home again, what they mean is you were never there*, which won the Michael Waters Poetry Prize. Her first poetry collection, *wine for a shotgun*, was published in 2013. She is the cofounder of *underbelly*, an online magazine focused on the art and magic of poetry revision.

Leslie McGrath is the author of three full-length poetry collections, *Feminists Are Passing from Our Lives*, *Opulent Hunger, Opulent Rage*, and *Out from the Pleiades*. Winner of the Pablo Neruda Prize for Poetry and the Gretchen Warren Award from the New England Poetry Club, her poems and interviews have been published in *Agni*, *Poetry* magazine, *The Academy of American Poets*, *The Writer's Chronicle*, and the *Yale Review*. McGrath teaches creative writing at Central Connecticut State University and is series editor of The Tenth Gate, a poetry imprint of the Word Works Press.

Richard Michelson's books have been listed among the Ten Best of the Year by the *New York Times, Publishers Weekly*, and the *New Yorker*. He received a 2016 Massachusetts Cultural Council Fellowship, the 2017 National Jewish Book Award, and the 2019 Samuel Minot Jones Award for Literary Achievement. Michelson's most recent collection *More Money Than God* was a finalist for the Paterson Prize. He served two terms as Poet Laureate of Northampton, Massachusetts, where he hosts Northampton Poetry Radio.

E. Ethelbert Miller is a poet, memoirist, and literary activist. He is an inductee of the 2015 Washington, D.C., Hall of Fame and a recipient of both the AWP 2016 George Garrett Award for Outstanding Community Service in Literature and the 2016 DC Mayor's Arts Award for Distinguished Honor. *The Collected Poems of E. Ethelbert Miller*, published in 2016, celebrates his poetry career of more than forty years. Miller's most recent book is *If God Invented Baseball*.

Kamilah Aisha Moon is a Pushcart Prize winner, finalist for the CLMP Firecracker Award and the Lambda Award, and a 2015 New American Poet who has received fellowships from Vermont Studio Center, Hedgebrook, and Cave Canem. The author of *Starshine & Clay* and *She Has a Name*, her work has been featured widely, including in the *Harvard Review, Poem A Day, Boston Review*, and *Prairie Schooner*. Moon teaches at Agnes Scott College in Decatur, Georgia.

David Mura has written four books of poetry—*The Last Incantations, Angels for the Burning, The Colors of Desire* (recipient of the Carl Sandburg Literary Award), and *After We Lost Our Way* (a National Poetry Contest winner)—as well as the memoirs *Turning Japanese* and *Where the Body Meets Memory* and a novel, *Famous Suicides of the Japanese Empire*. His latest book is *A Stranger's Journey: Race, Identity, and Narrative Craft in Writing*.

John Murillo is the author of the poetry collections *Up Jump the Boogie* and *Kontemporary Amerikan Poetry*. He is an assistant professor of English at Wesleyan University and also teaches in the low residency M.F.A. program at Sierra Nevada College.

Maria Nazos is the author of poetry, translations, and lyrical essays that have been published in the *New Yorker*, the *Tampa Review*, and elsewhere. She is the author of the poetry collections *A Hymn That Meanders* and *Still Life*. She has received fellowships from the Vermont Studio Center and the Virginia Center for the Creative Arts and a scholarship from the Sewanee Writers' Conference.

Marilyn Nelson is the author of *Carver: A Life in Poems, The Homeplace*, and *The Fields of Praise: New and Selected Poems*, which received the Poets' Prize, the PEN Winship Award, and the Lenore Marshall Prize. A professor emerita of English at the University of Connecticut, she has served as a Chancellor of the Academy of American Poets. She has been the Poet Laureate of Connecticut and has received many awards, such as the Frost Medal, the Ruth Lilly Poetry Prize, and the NSK Neustadt Prize.

Naomi Shihab Nye is a Palestinian American writer who lives in San Antonio, Texas, and has worked as a roving writer conducting workshops, readings, and poetry events all her adult life. She is currently on the faculty at Texas State University, and her most recent books are *Voices in the Air—Poems for Listeners* and *The Tiny Journalist*.

Cynthia Dewi Oka is the author of *Nomad of Salt and Hard Water* and *Salvage* (Northwestern University Press, 2017). Her work has appeared in *ESPNW*, *Hyperallergic*, *Guernica*, *Poets.org*, *American Poetry Review*, *Kenyon Review*, the *Massachusetts Review*, *Painted Bride Quarterly*, and elsewhere. Originally from Bali, Indonesia, she is a three-time Pushcart Prize nominee and a Leeway Foundation's Transformation Award recipient. She is based in the greater Philadelphia area.

Brenda Marie Osbey is a poet and essayist working in English and French. Her seven books include *All Souls: Essential Poems* and *History and Other Poems*. She is the author also of a Kongo–New Orleans opera triptych, including *Sultane au Grand Marais*. The recipient of numerous writing and research fellowships and awards, she is most recently the 2018–2019 Emilia Galli Struppa Fellow of the Virginia Foundation for the Humanities. The first peer-selected Poet Laureate of Louisiana, Osbey is a native of New Orleans.

Alicia Ostriker's most recent collection of poems is *Waiting for the Light*, for which she received the 2018 Jewish Book Council Award for Poetry. Ostriker is a chancellor of the Academy of American Poets and New York State Poet. As a critic, she is best known for *Stealing the Language: The Emergence of Women's Poetry in America*. She loves the ethnic mix on New York's Upper West Side, where she lives.

Willie Perdomo is the author of *The Crazy Bunch*; *The Essential Hits of Shorty Bon Bon*, a finalist for the National Book Critics Circle Award; *Smoking Lovely*, winner of the PEN/Open Book Award; and *Where a Nickel Costs a Dime*, a finalist for the Poetry Society of America Norma Farber First Book Award. His work has appeared in *The New York Times Magazine*, *The Norton Anthology of Latino Literature*, *Bomb Magazine*, and *African Voices*. He is currently a member of the VONA/Voices faculty and a Lucas Arts Literary Fellow; he teaches at Phillips Exeter Academy.

Emmy Pérez is the author of *With the River on Our Face* and *Solstice*. She is the recipient of a 2017 NEA poetry fellowship and is a member of the Macondo Writers Workshop. Her poem, "Not one more refugee death," is in honor of Gilberto Francisco Ramos Juárez and after "Vigil and Commemoration: Not One More Refugee Death," organized by the Human Rights Coalition of South Texas and held across the street from the border patrol center in McAllen in July 2014.

Marge Piercy has written the best-selling and classic novels *Gone to Soldiers*, *Braided Lives*, and *Woman on the Edge of Time*. Among her nineteen volumes of poetry, the most recent are *The Hunger Moon: New and Selected Poems, 1980–2010* and *Made in Detroit*. Born in center-city Detroit, Piercy is the recipient of four honorary doctorates. She is active in antiwar, feminist, and environmental causes.

Sasha Pimentel is the author of the poetry collections *For Want of Water*, winner of the National Poetry Series, and *Insides She Swallowed*, winner of the American Book Award. She has published in the *New York Times*, on *PBS News Hour*, *ESPN*, and *APR*, and she is the 2018–2019 Picador Guest Professor for Literature at Universität Leipzig, Germany. Pimentel is an associate professor at the University of Texas at El Paso, on the border of Ciudad Juárez, México.

Robert Pinsky was the United States Poet Laureate for three terms, beginning in 1997. A professor of English and creative writing in the graduate writing program at Boston University, he has earned many accolades as a teacher and poet, including being named William Fairfield Warren Distinguished Professor, the PEN/Voelcker Award, and the William Carlos Williams Prize. His anthology *The Figured Wheel: New and Collected Poems 1966–1996* was a Pulitzer Prize finalist.

Gabriel Ramírez is a queer Afro-Latinx poet. Gabriel has received fellowships from Palm Beach Poetry Festival, The Watering Hole, the Conversation Literary Arts Festival, and Callaloo. You can find his work on YouTube and in publications such as *The Volta, Winter Tangerine, Drunk in a Midnight Choir,* and *VINYL,* as well as in *¡Manteca!: An Anthology of Afro-Latin@ Poets* and *Bettering American Poetry Anthology.*

Luivette Resto was born in Aguas Buenas, Puerto Rico, but raised in the Bronx. Her first book of poetry, *Unfinished Portrait,* was named a finalist for the 2009 Paterson Poetry Prize. She is also a contributing poetry editor for *Kweli Journal,* a CantoMundo fellow, and the hostess of a monthly poetry reading series called La Palabra at Avenue 50 Studio in Los Angeles. Some of her latest work can be read in *¡Manteca!: An Anthology of Afro-Latin@ Poets.*

Peggy Robles-Alvarado is an educator with degrees in elementary and bilingual education and an M.F.A. in performance studies. She is a Pushcart Prize nominee, a Canto-Mundo Fellow, and a three-time International Latino Book Award winner. Robles-Alvarado is the author of *Conversations with My Skin* and *Homage to the Warrior Women.* She curated the anthologies *The Abuela Stories Project* and *Mujeres: The Magic, the Movement, and the Muse.*

Luis J. Rodríguez served as the Poet Laureate of Los Angeles from 2014 to 2016. His writings have appeared in the *Los Angeles Times,* the *Chicago Tribune,* the *New York Times, The Nation, American Poetry Review, Virginia Quarterly Review, Grand Street, Poets & Writers,* and other publications. He has written fifteen books of poetry, children's literature, fiction, and nonfiction, including the best-selling memoir *Always Running: La Vida Loca: Gang Days in L.A.* He is the founding editor of Tia Chucha Press, now in its thirtieth year.

William Pitt Root is the author of *Trace Elements from a Recurring Kingdom: The First Five Books of William Pitt Root,* and more recently, *Strange Angels.* His work has been funded by the Guggenheim and Rockefeller Foundations, the National Endowment for the Arts, and Stanford University. He is the recipient of three Pushcart Prizes, the Stanley Kunitz Prize, and other awards. He has also served as the John C. Hodges visiting writer at the University of Tennessee–Knoxville. He lives in Durango, Colorado.

Patrick Rosal is a writer, musician, and interdisciplinary artist. He is the author of *Brooklyn Antediluvian,* winner of the Lenore Marshall Prize. A featured performer across four continents and at hundreds of venues throughout the United States, he has received residencies from Civitella Ranieri and the Lannan Foundation, as well as fellowships from the Guggenheim Foundation, the NEA, and the Fulbright Program. He teaches at Princeton University and Rutgers University–Camden.

Joseph Ross is the author of three books of poetry: *Ache, Gospel of Dust,* and *Meeting Bone Man.* His poems have appeared in many places, including the *Los Angeles Times, Xavier Review, Southern Quarterly, Poet Lore,* and *Drumvoices Revue.* In the 2014–2015 school year, he served as poet-in-residence for the Howard County Poetry and Literature Society. He teaches English at Gonzaga College High School in Washington, D.C.

Nicholas Samaras is from Patmos, Greece (the "Island of the Apocalypse"), and, at the time of the Greek Junta ("Coup of the Generals") was brought in exile to be raised further in America. He's lived in Greece, England, Wales, Brussels, Switzerland, Italy, Austria, Germany, Yugoslavia, Jerusalem, and thirteen states in the U.S., and he writes from a place of permanent exile. His first book, *Hands of the Saddlemaker,* won the Yale Series of Younger Poets Award. His current book is *American Psalm, World Psalm.*

Ruth Irupé Sanabria's first collection of poetry, *The Strange House Testifies,* won second place for poetry in the 2010 Annual Latino Book Awards. Her second collection, *Beasts Behave in Foreign Land,* received the 2014 Letras Latinas / Red Hen Press Award. She works as a high school English teacher in Perth Amboy, New Jersey.

Lauren Marie Schmidt is the author of *Two Black Eyes and a Patch of Hair Missing; The Voodoo Doll Parade,* selected for the Main Street Rag Author's Choice Chapbook Series; and *Psalms of the Dining Room.* Her awards include the So to Speak Poetry Prize, the Neil Postman Prize for Metaphor, the Janet B. McCabe Prize for Poetry, and the Bellevue Literary Review's Vilcek Prize for Poetry. Her fourth collection, *Filthy Labors,* was published by Northwestern University Press in 2017.

Tim Seibles has received fellowships from both the Provincetown Fine Arts Center and the National Endowment for the Arts. Most recently, his book of poems *Fast Animal* was a finalist for the 2012 National Book Award and received the PEN Oakland Josephine Miles and the triennial Theodore Roethke Memorial Poetry Prize. He is a member of the English department and of the writing faculty in the M.F.A. program at Old Dominion University.

Katherine DiBella Seluja is a nurse practitioner and a writer. She invites the stories of her patients to inform her writing and strives to reveal raw and powerful aspects of health and illness in poetic form. She is a winner of the Southwest Writers Poetry Award. Her poetry collection *Gather the Night* focuses on the impact of mental illness. She is also the coauthor of *We Are Meant to Carry Water,* with Tina Carlson and Stella Reed.

Don Share is a senior editor of *Poetry* magazine in Chicago. His books include his translation *Seneca in English* and the poetry collections *Wishbone* and *Union.* He also edited *Bunting's Persia,* a 2012 Guardian Book of the Year and Paris Review Editors' Choice selection. His translations of Miguel Hernández's work, collected in *I Have Lots of Heart,* were awarded the Times Literary Supplement / Society of Authors Translation Prize and Premio Valle Inclán.

Danez Smith is the author of *Don't Call Us Dead*, winner of the Forward Prize for Best Collection and a finalist for the National Book Award. Danez is the cohost (with Franny Choi) of VS, a podcast sponsored by the Poetry Foundation and Postloudness. Danez's third collection, *Homie*, is forthcoming.

Patricia Smith is the author of eight books of poetry, including *Incendiary Art* (Northwestern University Press), winner of the 2018 Kingsley Tufts Award, the 2017 LA Times Book Prize, and the 2018 NAACP Image Award, and finalist for the 2018 Pulitzer Prize; *Shoulda Been Jimi Savannah*, winner of the Lenore Marshall Prize from the Academy of American Poets; and *Blood Dazzler*, a National Book Award finalist. She is a Guggenheim fellow, an NEA grant recipient, and a professor at the College of Staten Island.

Gary Soto has published more than forty books for readers of all ages, including *Baseball in April*, *Living Up the Street*, *A Summer Life*, *Buried Onions*, and *The Afterlife*. He is the author of "Oranges," the most anthologized poem in contemporary literature, and has been awarded fellowships from the Guggenheim Foundation and the National Endowment for the Arts. Widely translated, his books have sold four million copies nationwide. He lives in Berkeley, California.

Mark Turcotte (Turtle Mountain Ojibwe) is the author of four poetry collections, including *The Feathered Heart* and *Exploding Chippewas*. He was the winner of the First Annual Gwendolyn Brooks Open-Mic Award, and has received recognitions from the Lannan Foundation and Wisconsin Arts Board. He was the 2008 Visiting Native Writer at the Institute of American Indian Arts in Santa Fe. Since 2009 he has been teaching at DePaul University in Chicago, where he lives near the lakeshore with his wife.

Brian Turner's latest work, *My Life as a Foreign Country: A Memoir*, was called "a humane, heartbreaking, and expertly crafted work of literature" by Tim O'Brien. Turner's work has been translated and published the world over. His two collections of poetry, *Here, Bullet* and *Phantom Noise*, have also been published in several languages. He directs the M.F.A. program at Sierra Nevada College and serves as a contributing editor at the Normal School. He lives in Orlando, Florida.

Chase Twichell is the author of eight books of poetry, the most recent of which is *Things as It Is*. Her new and selected poems, *Horses Where the Answers Should Have Been*, won both the Kingsley Tufts Poetry Award from Claremont Graduate University and the Balcones Poetry Prize. She lives in upstate New York with her husband, the novelist Russell Banks.

Pamela Uschuk is the author of six poetry collections, including *Crazy Love*, which won the American Book Award, and *Blood Flower*, a 2015 Booklist Notable. Translated into a dozen languages, her work has received many awards, among them Best of the Web and the Dorothy Daniels Writing Award (National League of American PEN Women). Editor of *Cutthroat, A Journal of the Arts* and *Truth To Power: Writers Respond to the Rhetoric of Hate and Fear*, Uschuk is a Black Earth Institute Fellow (2018–2021).

Elisabet Velasquez is a Boricua writer from Bushwick, Brooklyn. Her work has been featured in *Muzzle* magazine, *Winter Tangerine, Centro Voces, Latina* magazine, *We Are Mitú, Tidal,* and more. She is a VONA Alum and received a fellowship from Poets House in 2017.

Richard Villar, born and raised in northern New Jersey, has been a longtime advocate for the Latino/a voice in U.S. letters. His work has been featured on NPR's "Latino USA" and has appeared in *Black Renaissance Noire, Hanging Loose, Beltway Poetry Quarterly, Amistad, Latino Poetry Review,* and the chapbook series Achiote Seeds. He directs Acentos, a grassroots project fostering communities around Latino/a literature. *Comprehending Forever* is his first full collection.

Ocean Vuong is the author of the novel *On Earth We're Briefly Gorgeous* and the poetry collection *Night Sky with Exit Wounds,* a New York Times Top 10 Book of 2016, winner of the T. S. Eliot Prize, the Whiting Award, and the Forward Prize for Best First Collection. Vuong's writings have been featured in *The Atlantic, Harper's, The Nation,* and the *New Yorker.* Born in Saigon, Vietnam, he lives in Massachusetts and teaches at UMass-Amherst.

George Wallace is the editor of Poetrybay.com, a coeditor of *Great Weather for Media,* and the author of thirty-four chapbooks of poetry in the U.S., U.K., Italy, Macedonia, and India. An adjunct professor of English at Pace University in Manhattan, he is writer-in-residence at the Walt Whitman Birthplace, and the recipient of numerous international poetry awards, including the Orpheus Prize (Plovdiv, Bulgaria) and the Alexander Gold Medal (Salamina, Greece).

Afaa Michael Weaver is the author of numerous poetry collections, including *The Plum Flower Dance: Poems 1985 to 2005; The Government of Nature,* winner of the Kingsley Tufts Poetry Award; and *City of Eternal Spring,* winner of the Phillis Wheatley Book Award. The recipient of the NEA and Pew fellowships, four Pushcart Prizes, and a Fulbright scholar appointment, among other honors, he became the first Elder of the Cave Canem Foundation in 1998. Weaver is alumnae professor of English at Simmons College in Boston.

Bruce Weigl is the author of more than twenty books of poetry, essays, and translations, including Nguyen Phan Que Mai's *The Secret of Hoa Sen.* He is the author of *On the Shores of Welcome Home.* His poetry collection *The Abundance of Nothing* (Northwestern University Press) was a finalist for the 2013 Pulitzer Prize. His work has appeared in such outlets as the *New Yorker,* the *Paris Review,* and *Harper's.* Weigl has been awarded the Pushcart Prize, fellowships at Bread Loaf and Yaddo, and a grant from the National Endowment for the Arts.

Eleanor Wilner's most recent books are *Tourist in Hell* and *The Girl with Bees in Her Hair; Before Our Eyes: New and Selected Poems 1975–2017* is forthcoming. Wilner's work appears in more than fifty anthologies. As a lifelong advocate for civil rights and peace, her awards include fellowships from the MacArthur Foundation, the NEA, three Pushcart Prizes, and the Juniper Prize.

Daisy Zamora is the author of numerous poetry books in Spanish, and several translated collections in the United States and England. Her essays, articles, and translations have been widely published, and her poetry appears in anthologies in thirty languages, including the *Oxford Book of Latin American Poetry*. Her latest poetry collection, *La violenta espuma*, was published in 2018 by Visor Libros (Spain). Her awards include the *Mariano Fiallos Gil* National Poetry Prize of Nicaragua, and a California Arts Council Fellowship. Featured in the recent documentary *¡Las Sandinistas!*, Zamora teaches at San Francisco State University.

About the Editor

Martín Espada was born in Brooklyn in 1957. He has published almost twenty books as a poet, editor, essayist, and translator, including his latest collection of poems, *Vivas to Those Who Have Failed* (2016). Other books of poems include *The Trouble Ball* (2011), *The Republic of Poetry* (2006), *Alabanza* (2003), *A Mayan Astronomer in Hell's Kitchen* (2000), *Imagine the Angels of Bread* (1996), *City of Coughing and Dead Radiators* (1993), and *Rebellion Is the Circle of a Lover's Hands* (1990). His many honors include the 2018 Ruth Lilly Poetry Prize, the Shelley Memorial Award, the Robert Creeley Award, the National Hispanic Cultural Center Literary Award, an American Book Award, an Academy of American Poets Fellowship, the PEN/Revson Fellowship, and a Guggenheim Fellowship. *The Republic of Poetry* was a finalist for the Pulitzer Prize. The title poem of his collection *Alabanza*, about 9/11, has been widely anthologized and performed. His book of essays, *Zapata's Disciple* (1998), was banned in Tucson as part of the Mexican-American Studies Program outlawed by the state of Arizona, and has been issued in a new edition by Northwestern University Press. A former tenant lawyer in Greater Boston's Latino community, Espada is a professor of English at the University of Massachusetts–Amherst.

CPSIA information can be obtained
at www.ICGtesting.com
Printed in the USA
LVHW091741271019
635473LV00003B/616/P